TOTALITARIAN RULE

TOTALITARIAN RULE

Its Nature and Characteristics

BY

HANS BUCHHEIM

Translated from the German by RUTH HEIN

With Annotations by KURT P. TAUBER
and the Translator

WESLEYAN UNIVERSITY PRESS

Middletown, Connecticut

I dedicate this little book to the memory of the ten Heidelberg classicists who lost their lives on an excursion on September 23, 1961, and most especially to the memory of my teacher, Hans Schaefer, and of my friend, Martin Friedenthal.

Contents

TOTALITARIAN RULE

1

Definitions and Comparisons

THE concept of totalitarian rule cannot be determined by purely logical means. It was explicated and clarified only by our own bitter experience with this form of government. As late as the end of the 1920's the word "totalitarian" was used to designate any state which was governed in an authoritarian rather than a parliamentarian manner. The London *Times*, for example, on November 2, 1929, spoke of a reaction against parliamentarism "in favour of a 'totalitarian' or unitary state whether Fascist or Communist"; the quotation marks and the explanatory phrase "or unitary state" prove that at the time the concept was still fairly unusual. In the 1930's and 1940's the experiences of the Third Reich and Stalinist Russia added to the definition the criteria of the synchronization *(Gleichschaltung)** and conformation of life, political police and concentration camps, and all the other horrors disseminated by these regimes. But admitting that in our century open terror has assumed particularly inhuman forms, such terror is nevertheless not confined to totalitarian rule and therefore is not sufficient to define it. From time immemorial despots

---

*Almost immediately upon seizing power, Hitler secured control over all public activities by abolishing the pluralistic and federal structure of the Weimar Republic. This "synchronization" of all previously semi-autonomous public bodies on the federal, state, provincial, and municipal levels was called *Gleichschaltung*. Later the term was extended to comprehend the incorporation into the Nazi control apparatus of all other hitherto independent organizations, clubs, fraternal orders, or professional associations. (KPT)

have imprisoned their opponents under particularly cruel conditions; they have tortured them, dishonored them, debased and executed them. The suppression of freedom has also always assumed the same forms. What Tacitus wrote in his biography of Agricola concerning the despotism of the Emperor Domitian was experienced as reality by the high school students of Hitlers' Germany:

"Not only [the writers] but their very books were objects of rage, and . . . the triumvirs were commissioned to burn in the forum those works of splendid genius. They fancied, forsooth, that in that fire the voice of the Roman people, the freedom of the Senate, and the conscience of the human race were perishing, while at the same time they banished the teachers of philosophy, and exiled every noble pursuit, that nothing good might anywhere confront them. Certainly we showed a magnificent example of patience; as a former age had witnessed the extreme of liberty, so we witnessed the extreme of servitude, when the informer robbed us of the interchange of speech and hearing. We should have lost memory as well as voice, had it been as easy to forget as to keep silence."[*]

The unique particularity of the unfolding of totalitarian power was at first experienced only by those who were under its immediate subjection, and even they understood it only gradually because it was an entirely new experience—at least in our century. Totalitarian power grows beyond all standards of normal politics, it gains incalculable and sinister dimensions; under its dominion life falls into confusion and insecurity of a kind not known heretofore. Human beings find themselves not only oppressed and confined in their freedom but also delivered up to the regime, mercilessly exploited by it,

---

[*]Tacitus, *The Life of Cnaeus Julius Agricola*, translated by Alfred John Church and William Jackson Brodribb, in *The Complete Works of Tacitus*, edited by Moses Hadas (New York: The Modern Library, 1942). The German translation used by the author differs in a few details but is substantially the same. (Tr.)

12

and finally, as it were inadvertently, criminally involved in the regime's activity. Characteristically, it was precisely the politically sophisticated observers who predicted a quick collapse of totalitarian rule, and from their point of view they were justified; for according to the traditional views and standards such a regime destroys all the preconditions that can give permanence to a government. Everywhere it goes against the most basic law of international diplomatic relations and economic life, destroys the ordered domestic government, openly goes back on its promises, at every step violates all loyalty and faith, is mendacious, unbalanced, repressed, unprofessional—nevertheless, totalitarian rule flourishes, secures its position, manages to win over large sections of the population though they resist at first, and can even place its opponents in its service.

Persons under totalitarian rule are always in the ranks, always under a strain. They may no longer show themselves as they really are but are constrained constantly to play prescribed roles in an atmosphere of false emotionality, joylessness, mistrust; and they must take care to put their loyalty "to the test." Not only does the regime forbid them to develop, but it seeks also to make of them other personalities than they are by nature; it not only restricts their freedom but tries as well to overpower them. This situation holds true for the declared adherents of the regime even more than for its opponents; for the adherents must always be anxiously concerned to move along whatever general line is currently in favor. No corner of public or private life offers refuge from control; one can inadvertently lay oneself open to suspicion anywhere. Applause, indignation, enthusiasm, willingness to serve are produced artificially. In general, artificiality is an outstanding characteristic of totalitarian activity, standing in grotesque contrast to the regime's favorite appeal to the authentic forces of life *(die elementären Kräfte des Lebens)*. But what is worse

is that concepts, words, and values are robbed of their traditional meanings, and moral standards become disordered. As
regards open terror, there is no doubt that it is to be abhorred;
but when evil appears in the guise of historical necessity, the
common good, the welfare of a people or a class, man becomes
prey to nearly insoluble moral conflicts. Thus, though dictatorial procedures, open force, and the deprivation of freedom
are also part of totalitarian rule, its true characteristic is the
creeping assault on men through the perversion of thought and
social life.

This assault follows from the fact that the totalitarian
claim to power is not kept within the bounds of possible governmental competence but—as the name makes clear—is intended to dispose *unreservedly* over the *totality* of human life.
The claim is not confined to the areas for which the state is
responsible but is allowed to encompass all areas, and to have
an exclusive voice even where the political regime can at
best play an ancillary role—as, for instance, in family life,
in scientific research, and in art. Totalitarian rule attempts
to encompass the whole person, the substance and spontaneity
of his existence, including his conscience. It does not acknowledge the primacy of society over the state as an area of freedom
which, in principle, lies beyond governmental control, but rather
interferes in it deliberately, to change it from the ground up
according to its own plan; for the regime wishes to create—
in accordance with its own ideological scheme and with social
engineering techniques—a wholly new society, a "new type
of man," as Lenin put it—even a new world. It undertakes
the production of an artificial, synthetic society.

Under these circumstances, men can have validity only
as building blocks or structural elements, raw material, "human
matériel"; totalitarian rule cannot as a matter of principle
acknowledge the citizen's personal autonomy, on which political
liberty is based, but must render him available for whatever

service seems desirable. While it is of the essence of the human personality in the last analysis not to be the available object but the partner of another human being, totalitarian rule attempts to make the unavailable accessible to itself. It destroys the old social elements and social processes and sets new, artificial ones in motion. Groups that are considered harmful are expunged; an attempt is made to form new elites, and there is no hesitation in modifying the personality of the individual by means of drugs and surgery. In this spirit the National Socialists were eager to create a new society by means of biological breeding and selection.

The totalitarian demand to create a new society was not restricted to bringing to power a new social stratum—the proletariat, for example, instead of nobility or the bourgeoisie— or to imposing new legal standards and institutional forms; such is the aim of *any* revolution and not a peculiarity of totalitarianism. *Totalitarian* interventions are directed to the basic forms of social life that arise directly from man's personal nature and political activity. Society is now no longer intended to emerge from the spontaneous unfolding of the individual; it may no longer be a network of relationships of freely reciprocal, cooperative, and oppositional activity (as it was defined by Theodor Eschenburg). It must now consist of a planned, mechanical continuity of functions; the place of free play is to be taken by a precalculated meshing of forces. A typical example of the fundamental character of totalitarian intervention is the circumstance that the Russian Bolsheviks were not content with the creation of a new marital law but believed themselves capable of abolishing altogether this basic institution of human life. It is no less characteristic, however, that this attempt failed because it amounted to an assault on the very nature of man.

Another example of how basic is the totalitarian demand to create a new society is offered by what is called indoctrination *(Schulung)*. In contrast to education, which presupposes a spontaneous and free unfolding of the human person and which first of all furthers and regulates such development, indoctrination is training toward specific modes of thought and conduct that are predetermined and can therefore be calculated to fit a particular function. In other words, indoctrination is a sociotechnical tool. The successfully indoctrinated person is prepared with prefabricated answers to all questions directed at him, and he reacts to certain stimuli (such as "capitalists" or Jews) in clearly foreseeable ways. He sees the world exclusively from the point of view and in the light of the ideology and is therefore able in each situation to act on his own initiative in whatever way is required by the consequences of the system. Thus he is—as it were—intellectually and morally synchronized with the practical course of the totalitarian exercise of power. While education presupposes a personal relationship of human equality between the teacher and the pupil, the person to be indoctrinated is degraded by the "indoctrination leader" to the object of systematic intellectual transformation.

According to Martin Buber, a society is humane to the extent that its members confirm each other. He considers its basis to be man's desire to be confirmed as what he is and his ability to confirm his fellow men in the same way; in this "reciprocity of realization" the growth of the self takes place. Willingness to influence *(Einflusswille)* in this case is taken to mean allowing the growth of whatever *must* be rooted in the substance of the Other, in the form suitable to it. Conversely, the totalitarian claim to power, in its preoccupation with utilization, is said to insist on treating people like objects, never establishing a relationship with them but eager to rob them of their independence.

The demand of totalitarian movements to dominate completely over men and societies without any controls and to re-create social life radically rests on their claim to know the intention of world history and therefore to be in the position of completing its course. Communism and National Socialism both grew out of the concept that the existence of a class and a people respectively was threatened, not by any constellation of political powers—which might have been overcome through available political opportunities—but by historical dangers, as it were: the suppression of the proletariat by capitalism, the dilution of the "blood" strength of the Nordic race through Judaism. It was believed in both movements that they stood at the pivot of world history, and they considered themselves chosen to bring about, by means of political measures, the "turning point" that they felt to be due.

The ruthless exploitation of large sections of European labor during the last century gave rise to the Communist insistence on changing the basis of social conditions and creating a new world in which want would be abolished and worldly goods would once and for all be apportioned fairly. Scientific knowledge of natural laws and the course of world history to this point did in fact seem to furnish men with the means of bringing about the desired condition and of creating a life of immutable freedom. The National Socialists explained Germany's defeat in the First World War and its consequences by the theory of the racial-biological decay of Nordic man, who was taken to be the creator and carrier of all culture. The "nordification" *("Aufnordung")* of the German people and the eradication of subversive Judaism were considered to create the necessary pre-conditions for the "thousand-year Reich" of the Germans and therefore for the final supremacy of the Nordic race.

The particular form of the Communists' totalitarian claim to control rests on the conception that the world can be known without lacunae, that such knowledge can readily be translated into practice, and that man has the right to enforce the actuali-

17

zation of the theoretically known on his fellows. According to the teachings of dialectical materialism, all of reality can be represented rationally in a closed system; this means that there is no transcendence at whose frontiers the human spirit will be caught between two truths. It is even believed possible to explore the entire world with such scientific exactitude that the relationships among things can not only be grasped and understood but can also be proved, and that in this way men can gain guidance for changing the world rationally. Marxism-Leninism comprehends itself as a sort of diagram of a wholly accessible world and thus corresponds to Marx' exhortation that it is not enough to interpret the world, but that it must also be changed accordingly. And whoever considers himself thus the sole possessor of the complete truth must necessarily feel himself duty bound no longer to accept the still incomplete actuality of the world and social life but to re-create it according to the truth; and if there is no other way, to force mankind to be happy and accept the truth. Thus, for example, Lenin was convinced that labor, with its narrow view of its conflict with the entrepreneurs, was unable by itself to develop a proletarian class consciousness, that such a consciousness required a perspective on historical development of which only an avant-garde of intellectuals was capable. These men, then, had the duty, in Lenin's own words, "to implant from the outside in the worker" the correct class consciousness.

In contrast to Marxism-Leninism, National Socialism was anti-intellectual. It glorified the life force, basic drives, blood; it considered intellect as the "opponent of the soul," according to the title of a well-known book by Ludwig Klages. The National Socialist claim to control the world did not appeal to reason, which perceives all and orders it anew according to objective truth, but to will, which heroically defies the powers that be, subjugates them, and shapes them after its

18

own subjective image. The "new German" wished to rule over fate, not in order to lead mankind into a condition of immutable happiness, but to take in hand *his* fate or that of *his* people in a struggle against the others, who were considered evil or too weak and who must therefore be justly destroyed.

Hitler held that to see the weak protected from the strong was enough to make one lose faith in divine justice. "The essence of National Socialism does not lie in its program but in its will," reads an editorial in the *Völkische Beobachter* of November 4, 1930; and Heinrich Himmler, the "Reich Leader of the SS," styled the will as that which is most sacred in man. Because it was claimed that Hitler fulfilled the vital law of the German people, his personal will as Führer was granted the right of unrestricted realization. Totalitarian subjectivism, the unlimited claim of a single person to dominate an entire people, found its undisguised expression in the sentence, "Hitler is Germany—Germany is Hitler." Since the authentic will of the people manifested itself solely in the will of the Führer, Hitler could also act "against the subjective opinions of individual members of the nation *(Volksglieder)* and a misguided popular mood." On this point, then, the National Socialist concepts led to the same practical ends as did the Communist ones: the totalitarian regime imposes on the people what is allegedly the people's real will.

In contrast to Communism, however, National Socialism granted only a subordinate role to ideology by placing it in the service of will. This will was not limited to the area framed by theory but was entirely free in its manifestations. It was not the task of the ideology to prescribe for will, but only to supply the firm bases of conviction, of belief, from which could arise the spiritual energies to get its way. Marxism and Communism wished to abolish religion and set science in its place. To the National Socialists, the ideology *(Weltanschauung)* was the new faith, better suited than the "old" Christian one to

19

aid the right to ascendancy of the stronger. With characteristically totalitarian behavior, they provided themselves with a substitute religion suited to their political needs. They made God manipulatable by equating Him with man's "inner voice" (the "voice of blood"); the Providence so often appealed to by Hitler was identified with his will.

Marxism-Leninism takes God more seriously than did National Socialism, which was in the tradition of bourgeois-liberal indifference to religion. Marxists know that if God exists, the world is no longer accessible to unlimited calculation and manipulation; therefore they must deny Him. National Socialists, on the other hand, did not experience the existence of God as a hindrance; He was one of the many unknown forces that had to be mastered in one way or another.

An aspect of the National Socialist ideology can be immediately compared in function with Marxism-Leninism, and that is racial doctrine. For it, too, is ostensibly scientific theory concerning historical and social processes, according to which the means of biological social engineering can be applied to the creation of new social conditions.

The totalitarian claim to sole control, which not only limits the individual in his free development but also forces him into the scheme of a planned world and thus overpowers him, contains in its essence an offer that corresponds to one of man's deeply rooted yearnings: the desire for a closed intellectual system, based on simple suppositions, which explains all existence and offers the guarantee of being able to cope with fate. In spite of everything man must endure precisely because he is subjugated by a system, he nevertheless succumbs to its demands, which promise release, and therefore develops loyalty and endurance as well as repeated readiness to accept empty promises. This is the reason why the totalitarian regime does not collapse even though it constantly violates the bases of normal political activity. Man's craving to be master of his fate allows him to accept—at times even enthusiastically to support—matters which, as he himself senses, overwhelm his core. Here is one of the strange inner contradictions of life under totalitarian rule, which cannot be understood from outside and through the categories of normal political reasoning.

Thus *totalitarian rule* is the demand for unlimited control over the world and hence social life, translated into political action; its organization and methods are distinguishing marks of the second order. Thus, for example, the laws against private property and freedom of movement, as well as the blockage of news sources from abroad, serve to make the subjects more accessible to the regime, although these restrictions taken singly are not elements essential to the definition of totalitarian rule. It is revealed as a form of government of a particular sort, not merely a variant of classical tyranny—a tyranny, as it were, with the methods of modern social engineering. This point can be seen in part in the role that planning plays in totalitarianism. Totalitarian government does not plan in order to rule more effectively; rather, it must be despotic in order to carry through the encompassing plan of constructing a new society.

Equally, the concept of totalitarian rule must be very clearly distinguished from those of *dictatorship* and *authoritarianism*. That these three concepts are nevertheless generally and superficially applied as though they were identical causes much confusion in political discussion.

Dictatorship is a legitimate aspect of republican constitutions. The ancient Roman Republic in times of acute danger named a dictator, who was vested with unlimited powers and who was not required to account for his administration as the ordinary magistrate was compelled to do; however, his term of office was limited to a maximum of six months. The provision of dictatorship is equally present in contemporary democratic republics; when a state of emergency requires the quick and vigorous concentration of the means of power of the state and the energies of the people, separation of powers and democratic procedures are temporarily suspended and the president or premier is given special authority. Thus, for example, the well-known Article 48 of the Weimar Constitution enabled the Reich President to be invested with temporary dictatorial power.

An *authoritarian* regime is a dictatorship without temporal limits. The democratic constitution is not rescinded temporarily but annulled altogether. A clique or one man freely disposes of the national means of power and issues decrees at will. In contrast to totalitarian rule, however, the authoritarian government remains within the framework of feasible national jurisdiction. Though within this framework the regime acts totally autocratically, it aims neither at fulfilling world history nor at creating a "new type of man"; rather, it leaves in effect the basic forms of social life and the consequent categories of values. Authoritarian rule will not always allow the individual to act according to his conscience, but—in contrast to totalitarian rule—it does not aim at exercising unrestricted control over his conscience. It is therefore in principle reconcilable with the practice of the Christian faith or with an independent morality, whereas the totalitarian ruler cannot possibly tolerate such manifestations. For by doing so he would set free the sources of man's inviolability. Hannah Arendt has appropriately pointed out that authoritarianism merely limits freedom, while totalitarianism aims at abolishing it. Authoritarian rule is the utmost limit of what a state can seize in the way of power without losing its character as a state. Thus, though it is a regression from liberal democracy, authoritarianism is not inhumane in its essence.

Of course each totalitarian regime is at the same time authoritarian and dictatorial, but an authoritarian regime need not be totalitarian, nor a dictatorial one authoritarian—not to mention a form of government with authoritarian overtones, which is entirely possible within the framework of a democratic constitution as the personal style of a statesman. There are not a few, however, who in all seriousness label such a style as "totalitarian" and marshal parallels with genuine totalitarian rule.

Many restrictions and infringements of political freedom which today are often found listed among the distinguishing features of totalitarian rule are in fact characteristic of all authoritarian regimes and, taken alone, do not therefore permit conclusions about the presence of totalitarianism. This holds true, for example, for the suspension of a democratic constitution, the elimination of parliamentary rule, mass marches organized by the military, and the single-party system. Only when this one party claims for itself the people's moral education and attempts to subjugate individual consciences does the transition from authoritarianism to totalitarianism occur. Even internment of political opponents is not in itself totalitarian; it becomes so only when it serves to break the prisoners' spirit and to exploit their labor—when, in other words, the concentration camp is used as an "indoctrination camp," a work camp, and a place of torture.

The essence of *fascism* is rebellion against freedom. Mussolini himself formulated this clearly and exactly in 1924 in the magazine *Gerarchia:* "All those who have not become victims of dogma hold it today as an irrefutable truth that mankind is tired of freedom. Man has made an orgy of freedom. Freedom is no longer the austere, chaste virgin for whom the generation of the beginning of the previous century fought and died. The fearless, bold, restless, hard youth which marches in with the dawn of a new era in history knows other words,

which exert a far greater charm: order, obedience, discipline.
. . . . Fascism . . . has once before marched over the decayed
corpse of freedom, and it will, if necessary, do so again." This
revolt against freedom could be heightened into a cynical,
inhumane hatred of freedom, into a disgust with freedom;
it characterizes all movements between the two world wars
which either called themselves fascistic or were properly designated as such. Among their adherents there were, it is true,
many who honestly believed that they *must* sacrifice freedom
because a free state was no match for the Communist danger;
others were blind to the value of freedom.

The revolt against freedom was also directed against everything vitally connected with it—the ideas of progress and
humanity, individualism and democracy. The Fascists therefore turned against both the bourgeois world and revolutionary
socialism, which appealed to the same ideals of freedom though
with different aims. Mussolini's *"fasci di combattimento"** and
the German *"Freikorps"*† also fundamentally rejected bour-

---

*Determined to organize his own political movement, Benito Musso-
lini, together with fifty to one hundred followers, founded in March 1919
the first *fascio di combattimento* (Combat Group) in Milan. In the following months, similar groups sprang up in most of the cities and towns
of Italy. Within two and a half years their militancy and terroristic activities gained sufficient popular support, as well as the tacit approval of
the military and the police, to enable Mussolini to take over the government. After the seizure of power and the consolidation of the one-party
regime, the *fasci di combattimento* became the Fascist Party organizations
at the grass roots, each commune forming its own *fascio*. (KPT)

†The revolutionary situation in Germany in the winter of 1918 spawned
a large number of military volunteers corps *(Freikorps)* whose counter-
revolutionary activities attracted radically nationalist officers and ad-
venturists. At the same time it was these "privately" organized combat
units that protected the Reich borders against the incursions of Polish and
Bolshevik troops until regular army units could be formed. Later, the
Volunteer Corps gave birth to a host of paramilitary, militantly anti-
republican, and stridently nationalist fighting leagues which were instru-
mental in the destruction of the hated Weimar regime. (KPT)

24

geois society, though they defended it against Communism. In their view, capitalism was the possessors' orgy of freedom, as socialism was that of the proletariat; both were created by the destruction of the "old bonds" and both threatened to destroy those bonds altogether. "Seen in this sense, capitalism and socialism are contradictions of a subordinate order, they are two sects of the great Church of progress," wrote Ernst Junger in 1930 in his essay "Die Totale Mobilmachung" ("Total Mobilization"). To understand fully this two-front opposition, we must recall that in the 1920's, during which the fascist movements developed, Communism had not yet revealed itself as a totalitarian system—which in truth offered enough "order," "obedience," and "discipline"—but seemed the advocate of unrestricted freedom, categorically denying any sort of order and commitment.

It is significant that the word "fascism," derived by Mussolini from *"fasci,"* means nothing more than "combat-group ideology," and thus offers no testimony concerning either the combatants' intellectual position or the pros and cons of their struggle. This is in contrast to Marxism, for example, which is a very particular doctrine that occupies an exactly locatable place in European intellectual history. The fascist interest in a positive intellectual, ideological, and philosophical orientation of the struggle took second place. In any case, it was not, as among the Marxists, a condition of engagement; under certain circumstances Fascists could forgo ideology altogether and find satisfaction in pure soldiering, heroics, and sheer activism. To the excessive Marxist demands on reason they opposed its undervaluation. They appealed to the creative *élan vital* as such, demanded action pure and simple, fought for the sake of fighting. The results of creativity and action, the aims of the struggle, on the other hand, were of secondary importance for them.

Mussolini wrote in 1926: "In that harsh and metallic word, struggle, reposed the entire program of Fascism as I dreamed of it, as I wished it, as I created it." Fascist ideologies are therefore lacking in that commitment to an intellectual concept and in the absoluteness of its orienting powers with which Marxism is able to create genuine revolutionary feeling and time and again to exert an intellectual attraction. The fascist ideologies rest only on a few more or less arbitrary absolutisms, which result in nothing more than rabid willfulness. They are romantic in the sense of Carl Schmitt's definition— that is, occasional;* the choice of objective and its intellectual execution follow not objective necessity but subjective whim. For this reason fascist ideologies are almost unavoidably extravagant and—like fascist organizations and symbols—appear exaggerated, out of proportion; they vaccilate unpredictably between the ridiculous and the unthinkably barbarous. Even when they accidentally hit on the truth, they lack, with few exceptions, any intellectual distinction. Fascism could take the direction of socialism (the "socialism of the trenches"!)† or the corporate state, Christianity or anti-Christianity, folk-

---

*Carl Schmitt, the outstanding political theorist of the anti-parliamentary, radically nationalist and etatist Right in the Weimar Republic, defined political romanticism by its necessary rejection of causal connections in favor of the relationship between an occasion and its consequences. According to Schmitt, for the romantic all concepts are mere occasions for the productivity of the creative ego. (KPT)

†For the development of a nationalist "socialism" the experience of the First World War was crucial. The front-line trench, insofar as it subordinated the claims of the ego to the needs of the group, became for the nationalists the great teacher of "socialism." There they learned the joy of subordinating themselves, their comforts, and their self-interests to the larger demands of the community; they tasted the exhilaration that comes from concerted action under unambiguous leadership for a supra-individual, collective goal. It was this experience of "socialism" which the young revolutionary nationalists brought with them from the front lines and with which they later destroyed the particularist pluralism of the liberal-parliamentary Weimar regime. (KPT)

ism* or etatism, Roman Catholicism or Prussian Lutheranism—
at heart it remained romantic and inimical to liberty.

Though a nationalistic orientation—generally in combination with imperialist demands—is found among all fascist movements of the 1920's, that is nevertheless not a definitive trait. The sole function of nationalism is to oppose the solidarity of all mankind, which is part of the idea of freedom, with another, more narrowly limited one. The nation was suited to this end, according to the political concepts of the 1920's; the later development in the Third Reich, however, demonstrated that this function could be transferred to the race. Thus, for example, the Germanic SS *("Germanische SS")*† was without a doubt fascist; it could nevertheless nurture a genuine internationality because it had discovered the "Germanic community" as a new form of limited solidarity. For

---

*The roots of this movement of thought lie in the romantic, quasi-egalitarian populism of the early nineteenth century. Folkism was the result of searching beyond the political and social springs of national unity for the substratum of Germanism, for the ineffably and quintessentially Teutonic. At the core of the folkish conception is the conviction that man's characteristic endowments derive from the ethnic group into which he is born, and that the groups, tribes, and races can be hierarchically ordered according to their intrinsic worth and cultural achievements. On both counts, the Germanic racial folk was said to represent the highest manifestation of the human spirit. (KPT)

†The Germanic SS was a concept dear to the imagination of both Hitler and Himmler, who saw the future in terms of a Germanic Reich, ruled from Berlin, as the core of a Germanic World Empire. Neither left any doubt that the pan-Germanic ideal was to reflect German domination and the political absorption of other "Germanic" peoples. As pro-Nazi but intensely nationalistic elements in the occupied countries of west and north Europe saw no reason to fight for purely German national goals, recruitment into the Germanic SS from the Low Countries, Alsace, Denmark, and Norway proved disappointing and inadequate. Under the impact of the manpower needs following the invasion of Russia, the concept of the Germanic Reich was replaced with the notion of an anti-Bolshevik political union of European states and an integrated European Army. Correspondingly, the Germanic SS gave way to national formations under native officers, the so-called Germanic Legions, within the Waffen-SS. (KPT)

the same reason, in the present day a fascist International can exist under the banner "Nation Europe."*

Because their ideologies lack intellectual conviction, fascist regimes can be greatly influenced by outward circumstances in the actual shaping of their rule. Should they encounter an indeologically solidly established society or strong political opposition, they remain content with relatively minor changes. If they encounter no obstructions, then their own lack of a principle that is capable of shaping the social structure and that would thus set limits allows them the unlimited radicalization of their "ideas" and the transformation of their "values" into absolutes. In short, though Fascism contains the tendency to a totalitarian claim to power, it is not—unlike Marxism-Leninism—determined on such a course; rather, it can find fulfillment within the limits of authoritarian rule. In Germany it was the lack of political substance, our people's fanatic desire for an absolute, and Hitler's totalitarian subjectivism that allowed National Socialism, as the only one of the fascist regimes, to become markedly totalitarian. Though

---

*The phrase Nation Europe is one of the few new ones in the postwar vocabulary of some former European Fascists and Nazis. Connoting a federated nationalist and authoritarian Europe as a Third Force, equivalent and equally opposed to the other two continental superpowers, the idea of a Nation Europe is primarily nourished by an intense anti-Americanism and anti-Communism. Moreover, the concept serves some nationalist groups as a common platform in their attempts to organize an international of nationalism. These efforts have gained literary and ideological support from a monthly entitled *Nation Europa* which, despite its limited circulation of some 8,000, has since 1951 provided a welcome forum for Nation Europe enthusiasts. Ideologically the notion of a Nation Europe derives partly from the old competing Waffen-SS conceptions of a racist Germanic Reich and an anti-Bolshevik pan-Europe, and partly from the newly won geopolitical insight that in the postwar era of continental superpowers, nations that refuse to join in opposition to liberal democracy and Communism are condemned to become either satellites or victims of the two superpowers. In Germany the Nation Europe idea has also been supported by the argument that reunification can be achieved only within a framework of neutralization, not merely of Germany, but of the entire European continent. (KPT)

Mussolini's fascist ideology showed many totalitarian traits, these had difficulty gaining a foothold among the political realities of Italy. Franco's regime clearly developed in an authoritarian direction and in the process increasingly shed its fascist traits. A form of authoritarian rule which from the outset lacked any fascist character is that of Salazar.

It is not a matter of hairsplitting apologetics but fact grounded in the intellectual amorphousness of fascism itself that the actual fate of freedom under the several fascist regimes differed so markedly. Anyone who fails to make these distinctions by examining the actual circumstances of each case, but simply concludes from a government's fascist design that it is totalitarian, inescapably approaches the Communist definition of fascism, which calls all anti-Communist political activity "fascist" and equates it with National Socialism.

If analogues are desired, Marxism and fascism on the one hand belong together as two examples of political movements; on the other hand stand authoritarian and totalitarian regimes as two forms of political rule. According to the first classification, National Socialism belongs on the side of fascism and must be seen in contrast to Marxism; according to the other principle, National Socialism and Communism both represent cases of markedly totalitarian rule, as opposed to those regimes, mostly fascist, which remain within the limits of authoritarianism. If it were to become a matter of deciding which of the two categories is the more important, formal observation suggests that greater importance should be granted to the differentiation of political movements than to that of forms of government. But since the totalitarian claim to rule transcends the horizon of political problems and touches on the roots of human existence, the common nature of this claim is after all doubtlessly the more significant one. In fact, National Socialism and Communism have much more in common in their totalitarian design and its consequences than do National Socialism and the regimes of Mussolini and Franco, in spite of common fascist traits. The Communist regime, in fact, in spite of its liberal-humanitarian pathos, abolished freedom just as much as did National Socialism, while Mussolini and Franco, in spite of their fascist expression, merely limited it.

Wherever the totalitarian claim to control is raised, it develops a superior efficacy, which gives largely the same complexion to Communist and National Socialist rule, while the differences arising from the Marxist and fascist origin retain an almost purely subordinate influence. Although there is the strongest imaginable contrast between the Marxist aim to lead all mankind into a state of definitive freedom and unalterable welfare and the fascist hatred of freedom, with its glorification of struggle, the totalitarian claim to power has nonetheless destroyed freedom in both cases. Whenever humanism takes no cognizance of the limits set for mankind, it leads to the same ends as antihumanism, which denies human freedom.

The activities of the political police did much to level the differences between the Communist Soviet system and the National Socialist rule by a Führer; for the unlimited power that both totalitarian regimes had to grant to the police necessarily influenced the whole structure of public life. Normal police activity is directed only against actual attacks on security and order and is strictly tied to valid laws. In this manner, not only are the citizens protected from encroachment, but the state itself is safeguarded against inadvertent changes as a result of extraordinary policy measures. In the totalitarian system, on the other hand, nothing limits the security task of the police; they are neither bound by the law nor forced to respect the inviolability of individual rights.

Though this approach confers unparalleled effectiveness on the police, it can have uncontrollable repercussions on the structure of the regime. For where an objective limitation of jurisdiction is lacking, there can be no objective limitation of responsibility. The chief of a police force freed of all restrictions can thus never fall back on the excuse that he has done everything possible for security within the framework of law and ethics; he may not rest until he has taken into account the final *conceivable* possibility of protection. Even if he himself were completely free of ambition and power drive, he would have to go all out to gain even the last key position and to eliminate the final suspicious character. And since he is bound to no standards, he will in the end—as happened in the Third Reich and in the Soviet Union—not limit himself to safeguarding the existing order but will try to bring about an order that offers the utmost possible security: the police state.

A similar development, it may be noted, obtains in the field of propaganda. To the degree that propaganda is freed from legal and moral restrictions, it will not be content with interpreting events but will attempt to bring about such events as are necessary to its purposes. An example of this point is the anti-Jewish programs of November 1938,* triggered by the minister of propaganda, Joseph Goebbels.

Very different significance and compulsion are ascribed by the two regimes to ideological doctrine. Marxist-Leninist doctrine, it is true, can be extensively interpreted according to the factor of expediency, so that the Communist policy of the moment can be represented not only as easily reconcilable

---

*Taking the assassination of a minor German diplomat in Paris by a seventeen-year-old Jewish refugee as a pretext, Goebbels, in the evening of November 9, 1938, ordered "spontaneous demonstrations" in the entire Reich. Under the ill-concealed leadership of the Party, the SA, and SS, thirty-six Jews were murdered, dozens of others seriously injured, twenty thousand were arrested, tens of thousands of Jewish shops and dwelling houses were looted and burned down, and hundreds of synagogues destroyed. Because of the two and a half million dollars' worth of broken window panes that covered many a German street in that night of horror, it became known as the "crystal night." (KPT)

with ideology but even as the only proper conclusion. On the other hand, it is impossible that different interpretations of the doctrine would be acknowledged to exist simultaneously within the same system; if differences of opinion arise, either one group must subordinate itself to the other or a split occurs. The struggle between different doctrinal positions, excommunication of "deviationists," purges along ideological lines are therefore characteristic of the Communist world. Before the October Revolution the greatest importance attached to the major conflict within the Russian social-democratic party between the mechanistic-passive tendency,* which was not revolutionary but believed it possible to wait until the predetermined course of history brought about the end of capitalism, and the dialectical-activist tendency, which demanded that the working class work actively for the destruction of capitalism. It was the triumph of this latter orientation, under Lenin's leadership, that raised to a maxim the totalitarian claim to disposition over history. Lenin properly appealed to Karl Marx, who had demanded the active transformation of the world in accordance with theory; but he changed the direction of that demand insofar as he enlarged into political activation of an ideology that which Marx had understood as application of scientific knowledge.

For National Socialism there was no pure, exclusively

---

*If one chooses to interpret the subtly and cautiously expressed relationship which Marx claimed to have discovered between changes in the modes of production and profound dislocations in the social structure in a vulgarly mechanistic or deterministic way, a kind of fatalistic quietism might well result. For if history moves in a predetermined and known path, those who bet on the "wave of the future" cannot possibly lose the wager: all they have to do is to sit and wait. That this determinist passivism rests on a total misreading of Marx is more easily recognized today than it was fifty years ago when Marx' early writings were either as yet unpublished or little known, when piety forbade distinguishing clearly between the thought of Marx and the contributions of Engels, and when the methodologies of the natural and the social sciences were still burdened with naïve assumptions as to materialism, causality, and certainty. (KPT)

binding doctrine, but only some standard concepts—such as "race," "Führer principle," "folkish new order"—for which basic recognition was demanded but for whose detailed interpretation great latitude was provided. The National Socialisms of a Göring, a Goebbels, a Himmler, a Ley, and a Rosenberg exhibited very different conceptions. No harm came of that, as it was this fascist regime's primary concern that one be willing and able to fulfill the will of the Führer. The commitment to Hitler was decisive—not, as in the Communist sphere, the commitment to doctrine. While Lenin furthered factual discussion on specific questions in order to discover the answers that were correct in the light of the doctrine, Hitler avoided any theoretical debate and saw in it only a danger to the unity and effectiveness of the movement. While the Communist Party brands and combats heretics in its own ranks on the basis of their theoretical utterances alone, Hitler took steps against followers with deviating views only when they refused him allegiance in the enactment of policy.

Thus from the outset National Socialism was a conglomeration of mutually antagonistic, conservative, national-revolutionary, folkish, social-Darwinist, corporatist, etatist elements of ideology, without its being possible to decide which among them represented the true National Socialism. Hitler made use of whatever variant he needed and disavowed it when it inconvenienced him; but nothing was further from him than to give official status to any one orientation. Even during the war he allowed to flourish the most diverse concepts of how a Europe ruled by National Socialism was to be shaped, and his followers could choose among Nordic, Germanic, national German, idealistically heroic, racially materialistic, and semi-Bolshevik interpretations of National Socialism. Hitler himself in his last years approached the view that National Socialism must be constructed on a scientific basis. But he considered this as almost a private opinion, and in any case he was far from persecuting those for whom National Socialism continued to be a "myth."

From the different evaluation of doctrine follows the difference of political indoctrination. The Communists placed in the foreground the imparting of knowledge, the National Socialists the shaping of a particular mentality. And their ideal—typically fascist—was the heroic fighter for the fight's sake, who "after the victory fastens his helmet all the tighter." But the self-reliance and the satisfaction with the preservation of decency, which are part of the hero's being, did not fit in with a regime that was desirous of ruling unreservedly over its human material and which constantly needed visible successes. The average man, moreover, is not in a position to comprehend the heroic ideal—much less to fulfill it. In the workaday world of the Third Reich, therefore, the ideal of struggle for its own sake was perverted into the practice of achievement for its own sake. To fulfill successfully and quickly an assigned task: that alone was what mattered, whether it was done by real ability or through cunning and unscrupulousness.

The final objective of Communist indoctrination is the mastery of the science of Marxism-Leninism and the ability to use the dialectic in order to derive the correct decisions for any situation and to convince the population of the necessity of the measures to be taken. But even this effort contains an excessive demand both on human reason as such and on the ability of most people for independent theoretical thinking. In practice, therefore, most discussions are sham, their results predetermined; again, one may steal a glance at those "above" to decide what attitudes are desired at the moment. Thus in the course of the years the science of Marxism-Leninism has become an article of faith, a substitute for religion for even the mass of the functionaries, and the actual everyday behavior is determined by the "socialist morality."

Hence, though the two regimes emanate from utterly different concepts of education, they come astonishingly near each other in the practical aspects of leadership, since both primarily demand faith, obedience, and efficiency.

The different ideological origins of the two regimes are still very noticeable in their styles, which, though they have no determining power, nevertheless are not without practical political significance. The apparatus, symbols, vocabulary, and expression of the Communists are unmistakably in the tradition of the socialist movement of the second half of the nineteenth century and under the influence of the positivist scientific attitudes as well as of the style of scientific discussions in the same period. If today the debate is only a sham debate and democracy only a façade, the Communist consciousness still retains the idea that the initiative must originate with the people and that each individual must be convinced of the necessity of the measures to be taken. It is considered indispensable to have action committees debate and popular initiatives demand matters that for all practical purposes have simply been ordered from above. Conversely, the National Socialists considered it necessary to put in the form of commands even the decisions that in practice were reached through negotiation and discussion. Their arrangements and symbols, their vocabulary and expression, originated in the "front experiences" of the First World War; on special occasions they pretended heroism, at work they deported themselves like soldiers, and on the whole they behaved and talked like men in the ranks *(Landser)*. Even musicians, actors, and art historians had to take care to impart to their activities the form of a tactical mission, whereas under Communist rule they must contribute in some way to production—or, recently, to peace.

Investigations into the success of National Socialism and the failure of Communism in Germany will reveal that, aside from other and admittedly weightier reasons, a contributing cause was the circumstance that to the German people the *Landser* mentality and militaristic thinking are more congenial than proletarian mentality and socialist thinking.

But on one point the regimes' differences in origin retained a decisive influence on their development. The total Marxist claim of reason led Communism into other ways than the fascist one of the will led National Socialism. In the Third Reich the final authority for all political decisions was Hitler's will, governed by his boundless subjectivity and unchecked by any objective control, not only de facto because of the existing power relationships, but in principle. The National Socialist regime was tailored to Hitler's person to such a degree, and the National Socialist ideology was so far lacking in power, that Hitler's untimely death would have resulted in a basic alteration of the regime; all the more so since all those leaders who might have assumed the succession were so dependent on Hitler's personal influence and so divided against one another that none could have asserted himself. But since fate allowed Hitler to complete his course, the peculiarity of the totalitarian absolute will could take full effect. That man who in an unbalanced manner is guided only by will despises reality, does not grant it any validity, but tries to force his subjective ideas on it. Though in specific instances he can beat a tactical retreat, he is unable to renounce his utopian aim to make reality submit to his subjectivity. The more he seems to succeed in such subjugation, the more he despises reality, overrides it, and will ultimately all the more surely be undone by it.

In the Communist realm, on the other hand, the highest authority is a doctrine, with objectively determinable and correspondingly valid content. Though the decisive leaders have wide latitude for personal decisions in specific cases, certain basic policy lines are firm; most important, doctrine prevents the dependence of the regime's continued existence for better or worse on the whim of a single individual. Even Stalin was forced to give his autocratic rule a Marxist-Leninist interpretation, and after his death the tradition of this doctrine proved strong enough to provide a basis for the policy of his successors and to prescribe for it a particular direction. No matter how far Marxist-Leninist doctrine distorts reality, it nevertheless does not despise it; it even appeals to it. For this reason it can adapt casuistically to objective conditions without breaking faith with its principles. The more actual power the Communists win, the less interested they are in the utopian elements of their originally totalitarian claim to power and the more realistic their policy becomes.

2

Life Under Totalitarian Rule

BECAUSE totalitarian rule aims at the impossible—to control man's personality and fate completely—it can be realized only in part. It is of the totalitarian essense that the goal is never reached and actualized but must remain a trend, a *claim* to power. The horror picture of absolute totality,* as some writers like to depict it, is a literary pastime, and it is dangerous to base one's considerations on it in the intellectual and political confrontations with Communism. Totalitarian rule is no uniformly rationalized apparatus, equally effective in all its parts. Such is the desired state, and in some areas the actuality may approach the ideal; but seen as a whole, the totalitarian claim to power is realized only in a diffused way, with varying intensity at different times in the different areas of life—and in the process, totalitarian traits are always mingled with nontotalitarian ones. But it is for this very reason that the effects of the totalitarian claim to power are so dangerous and oppressive; they are vague, incalculable, and hard to prove. It is always possible within the totalitarian realm to cite as many examples of harmless triviality as of satanic inhumaneness, and often both are inextricably fused in one and the same process. A German proverb has it that soup is never eaten as

---

*The German distinction between "total" and "totalitär" has here been retained, in spite of the general practice of translating both as "totalitarian," to accommodate the author's own distinction between the two; see page 97. (Tr.)

hot as it comes from the pot—and yet it has been ascertained that the soup is, in the end, a lot less digestible than it seemed when we ate it. Almost every observation made about a totalitarian measure has the fatal peculiarity of exaggerating the matter in some respects and of underestimating it in others. This paradox follows from the unrealizable claim to control; it is characteristic for life under totalitarian governments and renders it so extraordinarily incomprehensible to all outsiders.

The totalitarian regime superimposes, as it were, the grid of its ideology—the blueprint of the new society which it seeks to create artificially—on the old society, which is encountered in its natural basic forms, emerging directly from man's personal essence. But totalitarianism is able neither to eradicate the old society altogether nor fully to realize the new one. Thus a fusion comes about of the old natural and the new artificial actuality, which is all the more intricate and confusing as the regime often masks its true views and aims or reinterprets and twists into its own meaning traditional concepts and conditions. For example, the National Socialists purported to oppose only "political Catholicism," whereas in fact—and this was freely expressed in the higher official circles—they intended to exterminate the Christian religion altogether. They believed, however, that the mass of the German people were not "ideologically mature" enough to understand the necessity of the struggle against religion. The "reinterpretation" of the old social reality proceeds in such a way that the regime retains conventional institutions and concepts but invests them with a new meaning—or rather, with absurdity. This regime, too, has a party and elections and courts, but they are assigned functions entirely different from those they have in a free community. In the same way, there is much solemn talk of freedom, peace, progress, and democracy, but these concepts are detached from their original context, robbed of their traditional meanings, and overpowered by the new ideology. The concepts, as well as the people, are no longer allowed to be what they really are but must fulfill their assigned functions in a dialectical system.

The opponents of the regime refuse to recognize as a new reality the regimes' measures and concepts; they consider everything as nothing more than superficial "window dressing," which, as far as they are concerned, can be swept away again without any trouble. In the Third Reich there was much talk of the "brown nightmare"—which nevertheless was no nightmare but a reality and which incisively altered our lives. The followers and supporters of the regime, on the other hand, consider the old actuality as already conquered in principle and doomed to certain decline; such was the opinion held by Hitler concerning Christianity and the churches, and by the Bolsheviks—until recently—concerning bourgeois society. But both sides are in error and labor under illusions, for in fact two realities are simply dovetailed. H. G. Adler, in his work on the Theresienstadt ghetto, graphically illustrated this mutuality of two realities:

"It is risky, but it fits the conditions more closely, if we say that psychosis was rooted in the environment, for reality itself was schizophrenically split and disintegrated. Thus there existed a 'perverted' psychosis in the objective world; the subjective abnormalities were only its reflex. . . . Every value, every feature, every trait had sacrificed or altered its originally valid meanings. Since this was true even for the world outside the walls of the citadel, it applied all the more in the 'ghetto.' . . . It becomes comprehensible why visitors from the outside were deceived, for the truth could not become visible to a hasty visitor, since it remained elusive for the prisoners, who lived in the midst of the confusion. They were confused, confusion was imposed on them, and they themselves confused confusion further. The situation went so far that reality itself was often no longer considered present. . . . The degree to which

40

this process was achieved as a collective phenomenon is unique in the recorded history of man."

The true reality of the totalitarian system is a split reality; to put it another way, it is the fusion of the disturbed, partly denied, partly falsified, but nevertheless effective old reality and the extensively proclaimed but only fragmentarily and diffusely present new reality. Anyone wishing to live in accordance with actual reality must be at home in both realms— and not only as concerns what is overtly institutional, but even to differentiating concepts and ethical values. This means that conditions in the totalitarian sphere necessitate a way of life that can be called structurally conditioned opportunism. If reality is split, then of necessity many forms of behavior and expression must be ambiguous. This is especially true for any attempt to carry on effective opposition to a totalitarian regime. For the old real ty can make itself influential only if it speaks the language of the new one. Wherever the opposition is deprived of all legitimacy, it has to appear in the shape of agreement; the place of "No" must be taken by "Yes—but." This holds true even if structurally conditioned opportunism is hardly distinguishable from ordinary opportunism—which of course also occurs in excessive profusion—or even if the two are fused. A man would have to be a veritable Hercules in respect to character if he were not now and again to slip from one opportunism into the other. And we have all learned how easy it is subsequently to pass off opportunism as opposition, and to slander genuine opposition as opportunism. But this all but insoluble confusion is just one of those typical consequences of the unfolding of totalitarian power.

The individual and society are interdependent in such a way that society thrives on the spontaneity of individuals, who in turn require a constantly renewed impetus, provided by society, in order to develop. To the extent that the totalitarian ruler succeeds in getting society into his grip and subjugating it to his perverting plans, the consequence is unavoidable that the natural interrelations between the individual and society become poisoned and that therefore the individual's way of life is falsified at its very source. The regime is expert at exploiting in favor of itself and its purposes every spontaneous development of real skill and good will, all humane feeling and action. If in the Third Reich BDM girls* did volunteer work in hospitals or an SA member† helped a blind woman across the street, the action was praised as the fruit of National Socialist education. In the same way, the Communists consider a good movie, an athletic victory, a scientific discovery, or a technical invention to be testimony of the resolve to build socialism. A foreign visitor in Moscow cannot express his admiration for the Kremlin's old works of art or his gratitude for the helpfulness of his guide without having his words interpreted as an acknowledgment of Communism or a demonstration in favor of "peace."

A typical example of the manner in which the totalitarian regime exploits the normal social behavior of people in the narrow sphere of daily communal life is furnished by the Winter Relief Drive *(Winterhilfswerk)* in the Third Reich. The

---

*The League of German Maidens *(Bund Deutscher Mädel,* BDM) was the organization of the older girls (ages fourteen to twenty-one) in the Hitler Youth. Voluntary at first, later controlled by social sanctions, membership in the BDM became eventually compulsory. After the eighteenth year a BDM girl had to spend at least one year working on a farm or in a home or hospital. This was equivalent to the Labor Service of the young men, with only this difference: that the girls remained in the Hitler Youth throughout their work year and beyond, until their twenty-first year, while the boys graduated from the Hitler Youth into the Labor Service on their eighteenth birthday. (KPT)

†The Storm Troopers *(Sturmabteilung,* SA) grew out of the strong-arm guards that protected the earliest Nazi meetings into the uniformed street-fighting cadres of the Movement during its march to power. When these brown-shirted legions, under the leadership of Ernst Röhm, began to show signs of independence from the Führer, Hitler ordered the "Blood Purge" of the top SA leaders (June 30, 1934) and promptly reduced the once mighty army of the Movement to little more than a veterans' tradition association. (KPT)

National Socialists explained even the successful collections as a sign of the triumph of National Socialist persuasion in the entire populace; each gift was interpreted as a vote for the government. Anyone who consistently wanted to avoid casting such a vote would have had to refuse a contribution— but that would have meant behaving abnormally in the ordinary course of social life. For whoever consistently walks past all street collectors or does not give when solicitors come to the door will be considered at least eccentric by his fellow men's naïve social consciousness, which on the whole is unable to transcend the concrete individual situation; possibly in his fellows' eyes he has put himself wholly in the wrong.

This innocuous example demonstrates the basic form of a dilemma—which arose daily under totalitarian rule in the narrow communities of the office, the barracks, the evening classes, or wherever it might be—for those who recognize how the regime misuses for its own purposes the natural social behavior of its subjects. It requires uncommon self-assurance and great political and human tact under such circumstances to resist to the limits of what is possible at the time the regime's total claim, which is fragmented into the smallest routine demands, without at the same time offending against the naïve social consciousness of one's fellow citizens. The feeling of failing to measure up to such requirements is presumably much more often the reason for conforming than is the fear of surveillance and denunciation, which after all are generally in store only for pronouncedly oppositional behavior. Most people, in spite of inner reservations, will rationalize to themselves that they are unable to do otherwise than they are ordered. Once they have come to this decision, it becomes a question of very subjective and indeterminate judgment where each sets his limits of collaboration. This is especially true when the expectation is not of overt crimes but of small steps of cooperation, each of which taken alone is trivial and about which it is difficult to prove a degree of injustice. With all that, the tendency to be less than particular will be all the greater as "collaboration" is in any case possible only if one closes one's eyes to much of what goes on.

Thus the totalitarian regime uses the perversion of social activity to create conditions under which certain possibilities of evasion become impossible, not because they would be too dangerous but because they would lead to social absurdities in the personal sphere of everyday life. Conversely, normal conduct in the everyday world often results in a positive support of and a political commitment to the regime. Whoever has not experienced this process for himself, however, will have great difficulty in understanding the behavior of otherwise normal people under a totalitarian system.

Naturally a great deal is contributed to the maintenance of totalitarian rule by spiritual and moral human failings— intellectual laziness, ambition, cowardice, a lack of interest in the fate of one's neighbor. But the essential point, the unique trait, is the totalitarian ability to subjugate daily life and normal human behavior to its claim to power and to put them to its uses. Many of those who experienced the Third Reich as adults like to counter criticism of National Socialism with the observation that in those days there was also much that was good, especially much good faith and good will. This judgment is true insofar as it relates to the behavior of countless individuals: the soldiers who did their duty; the nurses who lost themselves in their work; the Jungvolk leaders*

---

*The German Young People (*Deutsches Jungvolk*, DJ) was the Hitler Youth organization for boys in the ages of ten to fourteen. From the DJ the boy graduated into the Hitler Youth (HJ) in the narrower sense, that is, the organization of the fourteen-to-eighteen-year-olds. Although in the first years of the Third Reich the styles of these two divisions of the Hitler Youth tended to differ due to the Youth Movement background of a large number of early DJ leaders, their influence was quickly reduced. Eventually made compulsory, both organizations stressed ideological indoctrination, physical fitness, and premilitary training. (KPT)

44

who took their groups on hikes without thinking of politics; the NSV officials* who really cared only about social welfare; and many others.

But the regime knew how to put all this devotion into the service of its inhuman purpose and thus to bring about terrible calamity. Whoever lives in a society which stands so to speak in the circuit of a totalitarian claim to power—indeed whoever merely comes in contact with it—becomes ineluctably involved in one way or another. Abstinence is as impossible to an individual as is his withdrawal from society without atrophying as a person. Man's normal expressions become falsified even as they arise, and what he says and does slips into frames of reference other than he believes or intends: it is precisely in these processes that the individual experiences the abolition of freedom in everyday life.

Under totalitarian rule, justice, like freedom, is not only violated and limited in its validity (which is in any case the order of the day), but it is altogether "abolished." It loses its absolute validity, without which its essence is unthinkable, and it is hedged about with reservations. Since the regime regards people as the objects of its measures, as human maté-riel, it denies the individual character of their being and with it the interior point of reference of every right. For human autonomy and dignity are, in this world, the crux of any right

---

*The National Socialist Public Welfare Organization (*Nationalsozial-istische Volkswohlfahrt*, NSV)—though on the face of it concerned purely with welfare—soon turned out to be yet another instrumentality of the control and socialization apparatus of the totalitarian regime. The NSV's ostensible prime concern was the care of the German family through its "Mother and Child Aid" division. But although its propaganda oozed sentimental humanitarianism, it could not conceal that its real function was to promote a rapid increase in the birth rate. Moreover, in performing the task that hitherto had been the work of hundreds of independent church, labor union, and social welfare groups, the NSV essentially served to extend public control over vast areas that had theretofore been relatively autonomous. (KPT)

worthy of the name; in them is rooted the inalienable right "with which we are endowed" and which we possess simply because we are human beings, whether we have earned it or not, whether we act according to our ability or not. This right the totalitarian ruler neither knows nor acknowledges. He confers only certain rights, as if they were privileges, on his subjects in accordance with their usefulness and achievements; he recalls these rights when someone proves himself no longer useful or reliable. Should it become apparent that someone is a "parasite" *(Schädling)*, he is not judged according to law and justice; logically, he falls prey to social disinfection and is exterminated.

Justice is further deprived of its absolute validity by the totalitarian demand to dictate history. For to the extent that history is not specifically viewed from ethical or theological vantage points (and such is not the case with the philosophies of history of the totalitarian systems), it runs its course beyond good and evil, right and wrong. The law of historical development is presented as valuefree and almost as a natural law. If man is to order his decisions according to such a law (since it is his wish to fulfill the meaning and course of history), the alternative of right and wrong can be of only secondary importance; primarily he faces the question whether a decision corresponds to the law of history or not. Alleged historical necessity is thus raised to the highest authority and takes precedence over legal standards as well as ethical laws. In matters of supreme policy the appeal to historical necessity at the expense of justice has always played a part when it was a matter of the vital interests of a state or a nation— whether rightly or wrongly is not the question here. What is new in the totalitarian realm is the regime's introduction of this rule even for everyday individual behavior, instructing the citizen to derive the criteria of ethical evaluation from the

46

alleged knowledge of the laws of historical development, as the Polish philosopher Lešzek Kolakowski once put it. Reinhard Heydrich, chief of the Gestapo, in 1936 unequivocally and unmistakably formulated the same axiom in a pamphlet entitled *Wandlungen unseres Kampfes (Transformations of Our Struggle)* as follows:

"To preserve our people, we must be hard on our opponents, even if we run the danger of perchance harming an individual opponent and of possibly being decried as unrestrained ruffians by a few no doubt well-meaning persons. For if, as National Socialists, we do *not* fulfill our historic task because we are too objective and humane, we will nevertheless not be credited with mitigating circumstances. It will simply be said: In the judgment of history, they did not fulfill their task."

National Socialist constitutional doctrine explicitly declared history to be the sole controlling authority over the Führer's actions. For him there was to be no accountability to parliament and no confirmation of the legality of his decisions through a supreme court; he must "prove himself through the historic task of the people." Werner Best in his 1940 volume, *Die deutsche Polizei (The German Police)*, expressed with particular clarity the abolition of the legal norm in favor of the law of history. At that time he wrote that it was no longer a question of law, but one of fate, whether the will of the leadership was correct; for genuine abuse of the constituent power *(Rechtssetzungs-Recht)* by popular leadership would be "punished by fate, more surely than by a supreme court, pursuant to the violated 'laws of national existence,' with misfortune and overthrow and failure in the face of history." The mere fact that as we read this sentence today we are reminded how horribly true it has proved among our own people shows that it is not lacking in a kernel of truth. A statesman has a kind of responsibility to history of which he is not relieved even when his decisions are covered by parliamentary votes and judicial decrees. But this responsibility is in addition to the legal, ethical, and political responsibilities and by no means rescinds them, as totalitarian doctrine holds. Neither the responsibility to history nor that to God as the Lord of history exempts the statesman from the duty to render an account to law and populace. But whoever considers himself in possession of the plan of universal history will naturally find it quite in order to disregard the autonomy of politics and the consequent responsibilities and to raise the presumed demands of history to the position of an exclusive norm.

The functionary who recognizes historical necessity as the supreme guide need not therefore have lost his innate feeling for justice; he may still be able to hear the voice of his conscience. But in a conflict situation, conscience will no longer be his highest authority; it will be "a private matter," which must retreat before historical necessity. From this standpoint, he no longer considers it quite so absurd that under certain circumstances he may be called upon to stifle the voice of his conscience and that such an act will be considered a moral achievement, as if it represented the conquest of a private weakness for the good of the common weal. In any event, the regime does not (at least in its proclamations) expect justice to be sacrificed to the ordinary aims of everyday life but only to such exalted aims of universal history as the "eternal life" of a people or the triumph of socialism or the Aryan race, as the case may be. If the regime were to promulgate only unadorned opportunism and naked brutality, it could not induce otherwise normal human beings to expose themselves to inner conflict, perhaps even to become criminals. Nevertheless, it will not take long for someone who has learned to silence his conscience for the sake of historical necessity to comprehend how he can lend his personal everyday aims the desired ideological interpretation.

48

The appeal to historical necessity played a major part in the destruction of the Jews as well as in the arbitrary killing of soldiers and civilians during the last weeks of the war. A whole series of orders and regulations made it clear to all who were receptive that in that historic hour, in which the life of an entire people was at stake, legal considerations were a sign of weakness and observance of procedural formalities bordered on undermining military discipline. Whoever in those days ordered an arbitrary execution never bothered to seek out legal justification. If today a judge inquires into such a justification, he is missing the point about the accused's intellectual position at the time. It was never thought that a foundation in law existed, but it was believed that none was needed and that everyone was released altogether from the necessity of legal considerations. The justifications were "security measures," "deterrence," and "setting an example." Thus Robert Jackson, the American chief prosecutor at the Nuremberg Trials, rightly observed: "I cannot, of course, deny that these men are surprised that this is the law; they really are surprised that there is any such thing as law. These defendents did not rely on any law at all. Their program ignored and defied all law."*

The significance of direct intervention in the personal core of man through "brainwashing" or biological breeding and extermination consists in the fact that such manipulations reveal the extent of the totalitarian claim to control at its most extreme. But in practice these processes seldom occur; it is more characteristic for everyday life in a totalitarian system that the regime brings the populace into line by the perversion of its daily circumstances and the falsification of its concep-

---

*Robert H. Jackson, *The Case Against the Nazi War Criminals* (New York: Knopf, 1946), p. 72. (KPT)

tual world. A favored and very dangerous device for this effect is the abuse of morality. Although the totalitarian regime is itself wholly amoral, it is nevertheless among its peculiarities that it constantly and pervasively preaches morality, appealing to the moral sense of its victims and thus harnessing them to its purposes. When it becomes a matter of translating into action alleged historical necessity, no standards are supposed to count but those of the totalitarian claim, for the accomplices are encouraged to ignore the voice of conscience even when committing the most dreadful crimes; but for the rest of the time the demand is for a positively scrupulous conscience.

Himmler, discussing the SS members entrusted with the systematic destruction of the Jewish people, once stated that he was proud of them because they had assumed this heavy task for the sake of the German people's future and nevertheless all but a few had remained decent persons, who had not misappropriated Jewish property. The systematic ten-thousand-fold murder is here no longer even perceived from an ethical and legal perspective. Objectively it is seen as historical necessity, subjectively at best as an extraordinary burden on the feelings and nerves of the perpetrators, since it is not, when all is said and done, a very nice business to kill masses of people. The moral qualification enters in only as concerns the petty theft at the edge of the great killing because it is evaluated as a lack of discipline. "Whoever takes so much as a mark," Himmler once said, "is a dead man."

The SS indoctrination literature was full of exhortations to loyalty, courage, honesty, gallantry, humility, and helpfulness; all these virtues are illustrated with edifying examples. Moral education therefore plays a major role. Nevertheless, the validity of these virtues was limited in such a way that they lost their substance and deteriorated into tools of the totalitarian regime. For in the first place virtues were cut adrift from their connection with truth; their value was measured only by their utility in enhancing the reputation of the organization, for example, or in raising the effectiveness of the troops. In contrast, no attention whatever was paid to the meaning that virtues derive from their relation to the true and the good, which determines their essence. Secondly, these virtues were deprived of their universal binding force. One axiom must have absolute validity for the SS member, in Himmler's opinion: "Honesty, decency, loyalty, and comradeship we owe to the people of our own blood, and to no one else."

The same concepts are found in Lenin's writings. In the autumn of 1920, in a speech to the Communist youth leaders, he rejected any morality derived from supernatural, supraclass concepts, branding them as deception and humbug; he claimed that Communist morality must have its source in the interests of the proletarian class struggle and must be completely subordinated to it. "We say: that is moral which serves the destruction of the old exploitative society and the rallying of all working people around the proletariat, which is erecting the new Communist society."

Just as legality is put at the disposal of expediency and the striving for power when it is cut off from its relation to the concept of justice, virtues become equally manipulable when their relationship to truth is blocked or destroyed. Moral energies are degraded into tools of the ruler and are placed in a situation of interchangeability with ideological arguments, technological measures, and man's vital instinctual energies. It then becomes a question of immediate need and expediency whether the regime will at any one time make use of the people's physical abilities, technical knowledge, ideological prejudices, particular virtues or vices, gallantry or hatred; for morality has lost any transcendent effectiveness. The same organization which appealed to soldierly virtues in the Waffen-SS* for the purpose of successful warfare cleared the ground in the concentration camps for the development of sadistic drives. The totalitarian ruler himself displaces the transcendent norm or conscience. The regime may be expressing a sober truth when it proclaims that it is man's moral duty to work. But in reality, the regime is not the proper authority to supervise compliance with this moral obligation; when it nevertheless arrogates this power to itself, laziness becomes a political felony.

No matter how severe and detailed legislation and bureaucratic regulations may be, they are unable by their very nature to realize the totalitarian claim in its complete boundlessness. For although each measure has specific application, such application is also always limited; in the very fact that it expressly declares certain achievements to be duties, it has the effect of declaring everything else not to be an unconditional obligation. The totalitarian ruler, however, wants to be able to make any desired performance appear as a duty, depending on the requirements of a particular situation. He relies for justification on elementary powers preceding any political order, such as the law of history or a people's right to survival; in the same way he again reaches beyond positive law to prepolitical commitments for the purpose of leading his subjects. In order to make men submissive and to circumvent such ethical guarantees as still remain, he appeals to

---

*The Armed SS (Waffen-SS) grew out of the formations organized to protect the person of the Führer and—following the Blood Purge of the SA in 1934—to guard the increasing number of concentration camps. Neither a regular branch of the Wehrmacht nor—like the General SS—merely a part of Hitler's terror apparatus, the Armed SS grew in the course of the war to almost one million men, half of them volunteers. Because most of the units were exceedingly well trained, often brilliantly led, and above all superbly equipped, they soon became known to friend and foe alike for their great military effectiveness. At the same time, their intense ideological indoctrination, their self-image as political soldiers and as keepers of the Holy Grail of Nazism, led the Waffen-SS to fight with unequaled brutality. (KPT)

moral and ideological obligations, to the loyalty of trusting followers *(Gefolgschaftstreue)*, to zeal for the building of socialism, to ideological conviction and love for the Führer, to national and class consciousness, willingness to serve, and a spirit of sacrifice. With these powers even that can be forced which is essentially beyond subjection to legal norm, and the energies thus released are greater than those growing out of simple compliance with legal duty.

Even a liberal state does not exist solely by virtue of the achievements to which it compels its citizens by law; it must also appeal to their initiative and sense of responsibility· Monarchy rests on something that the king cannot command, democracy on something that cannot be voted on but on which the citizens agree without a vote. When the base of common convictions is too small, when the citizens are unable to imbue public life with intellectual and moral content or are unwilling to go further than they are legally obliged—then the state is weak, perhaps its very existence is threatened. But such conditions belong in the area of freedom; the state depends on them without having the power to compel them if it is not to become totalitarian. Thus, it can exhort its citizens to make voluntary efforts, but it must allow each one the freedom to reject the appeal on the basis of the legal minimum requirement. Precisely because this state grants its citizens the right to refuse further demands than are required by law, it opens the possibility for truly voluntary action.

The totalitarian regime, on the other hand, cuts off this retreat into law, this right to limit oneself to the performance of inalienable duties, and in this way it turns an appeal to ethics into political coercion.

Thus is created what in the Third Reich was popularly called "voluntary coercion"—which is even more important in the Communist realm, since there greater weight is given to the demonstration of objective approval than was the case among the National Socialists. A few days before August 13,

1961, a Vopo* stopped a man on his way into West Berlin and asked him if he was aware that crossing the frontier was forbidden. To the counterquestion as to which law contained such a ban, the policeman answered that the law had not been promulgated yet, "but," he added, "don't act so innocent, you know perfectly well what's at stake."

According to the law, enrollment in the Waffen-SS was always voluntary. But the recruiting commissions got their men by arguing that whoever loved the Führer and was prepared to do everything in his power for the final victory could not refuse entry into the Waffen-SS; for no organization loved the Führer more than the Waffen-SS, and none fought so unreservedly for the final victory.

Even in the Communist-dominated countries the law grants everyone the right to cast a secret ballot in the elections. But if the populace, ostensibly from overwhelming love for the regime and boundless enthusiasm for its aims, proceeds to an open election, someone who uses the polling booth—relying on the letter of the law—casts suspicion on himself. This is the decisive point: in the totalitarian system, whoever appeals

---

*In the night of August 13, 1961, after the flood of East German refugees through West Berlin had reached a new high of four thousand in the previous twenty-four-hour period, border police and army guards, reinforced by tanks and armored cars, sealed off the entire Berlin frontier, and workmen began to erect barbed-wire fences with feverish speed. In the following weeks the temporary fences were replaced by a high and solid wall, and all but four of the thirteen crossing points that had been originally left open were closed off.

The People's Police (*Volkspolizei*, Vopo) of the German Democratic Republic is a uniformed, well-armed force that in addition to guarding the borders with West Germany provides protection for strategic factories, and is trained and used in riot control. Though ubiquitous and indispensable in shoring up the very unpopular Ulbricht regime, the Vopo is not a political police in the narrower sense. Typically, however, and along with the rest of the East German security apparatus, the Vopo is charged as much with detecting and preventing actions that might become dangerous to the regime as with restraining actions that clearly are contrary to existing law. (KPT)

to his legal rights in refusing to submit himself to the will of the political leadership is accused at the least of lack of political instinct, and probably even of nefarious intentions. When the entire populace is simultaneously swept up by a wave of enthusiasm, the same wave sweeps away all legal norms that still offer protection to the individual conscience against the grasp of the absolute claim to control. The individual finds himself forced to do more than is required by law, for any appeal to legality appears under such circumstances as reprehensible shirking.

The totalitarian regime thus controls its defenseless victims by replacing the strictly applicable laws with ethical demands, in the process setting itself up as the judge of good and evil. All legal and institutional regulations of the relations between government and the governed create not only duties for the latter but also a free area in which conscience is explicitly safe from the inroads of authority. The more this relationship is made an ethical one, and the more law and morality are commingled, the more the individual is exposed to the danger of moral constraint and finds himself compelled to perform actions against his will. Unfortunately, the general consciousness approaches this dangerous development even outside the totalitarian frontiers, whenever it condemns the essential formalism of the legal order and time and again expects the judges to penalize not only transgressions of the law but also moral deviation.

3

Excursus on the Concept of Politics

WHEN we speak of politics, we do not mean affairs of state as a whole; for example, we exclude administration. A political decision is different from an administrative decision, a minister is assigned functions different from those given to civil servants. In contrast to the man who holds a civil service job, the political actor may—indeed, should—take sides and take into account various interests and power combinations. While it is the functionary's job to apply the laws, it is the business of the politician to create laws, to decide on matters which are not yet regulated by law or which by their very nature cannot be regulated by law. Naturally the functionary also bears political responsibility, both in his capacity as a citizen and in the fulfillment of his office; the politician, on the other hand, is equally bound by the laws. The difference is rooted in their particular tasks: the politician shapes public life, the functionary provides public service.

This comparison makes clear three essential traits of political thought. First, politics is not directed simply to the facts concerning the problem in each case; it consciously and expressly also takes into account the conduct of those persons who are affected by the matter for good or ill, who resist or who welcome it, who stipulate conditions or who demand rewards, who feel injured, are reluctant to share responsibility for an enterprise, or whatever else may be. A characteristic question for the politician is whether what he actually wants is possible or can be made possible, given the particular conditions among his fellow men; he can be recognized by the fact that he starts out by considering factual problems from the viewpoint of the personal relationships that must be taken into account. But the active shaping of the conditions is more fundamental than consideration for the given circumstances.

This fact leads us to the second trait. A certain originality is peculiar to political action, a particular spontaneity and freedom of initiative—which, it is true, carries with it a greater personal responsibility and heightened personal risk. In its nature, political action is free. For man is not an animal which instinctively occupies its predetermined place in the herd; he himself determines his position in society and consciously assumes it. Human society is the result of individual decisions about position, freely taken though in practice always within the framework and under the influence of the system in power. For the freedom of political decision is not absolute. Though man is an original, independent being, he is nevertheless predisposed to and dependent on the society of his fellows. Though he does not derive his existence from the group, he is nevertheless dependent on it; he is autonomous but not self-sufficient. He seeks the community because without it he can neither exist materially nor develop intellectually, but at the same time he shuns it in order to find himself. From this conflict arises the basic tension of political life.

Thence the third trait follows: political action is connected with the group. Human thinking and doing become political when, deliberately or accidentally, they touch on society as such. It need not necessarily be the political community but can be the "society" of an association, a factory, a family; consequently, alongside national politics, there exist organizational politics, labor politics, family politics. But the true locus of politics is in the state because the state peculiarly serves the molding of the human community as such. All other groups (with the exception of the distinctive community of the church) exist primarily for material purposes or depend on nonpolitical bonds and are only secondarily political. The university, for example, serves scholarly research and instruction—university politics take second place to that purpose; the family rests on ties of love and blood—compared to these, family politics is also secondary; a factory serves the purpose of producing goods—labor-political problems are secondary and by no means represent the true purpose of the factory. Conversely, it is the purpose of the state to shape human community as such, while for the state all practical purposes and nonpolitical connections are of secondary importance. For the common weal is not a purpose for whose sake political order is established; rather, it has its existence within this order.

Aristotle wrote (*Politics*, 1253a) that man is more of a political animal than the bee or any other gregarious animal because he alone is endowed with the gift of speech with which he can express, not only pleasure and pain, but also the expedient and inexpedient and the just and the unjust; the association of living beings who have this sense makes a family and a state.* Thus political life has its immediate origin in man's spiritual and ethical existence, being the everyday manifestation of that existence, though it has its proper place only within the polity. That is why we understand the word "political" in its precise sense to refer to the polis (state), though we are aware that it designates an elementary form of conduct, present in all sectors of human life. But this precise sense is meaningful only so long as public life remains closely connected with our spiritual and ethical existence. This fact is easily forgotten in view of the complexity of the modern state's structure as well as the multiplicity of the tasks the state has assumed. Instead, the concept gains ground that

*This paraphrase follows the Benjamin Jowett translation. (Tr.)

statecraft and political activity are specialized disciplines among many others, which fall within the competence of a few specialists, while all others can allow the specialists to assume responsibility without themselves incurring injury to their human substance. Misunderstood as a specialized field, the concept of politics cannot help but lose its meaning.

Though freedom of political action is limited in practice by a network of previous decisions, these nevertheless always remain open to possible counterdecisions and can, when necessary, be countermanded. It is part of the essence of politics that it contains the freedom to make decisions against the existing order, even against earlier decisions of the same system. Nor does a decision lose its political aspect because it proceeds against law and justice or because it is amoral. For it is also of the essence of political action that it contains the possibility of deciding in favor of falsehood, evil, injustice—even of self-destruction. This state of affairs corresponds to man's freedom to believe or not to believe in God, to promote or reject his own salvation, to maintain or destroy his own life. For true freedom for all that is good can exist only if freedom is also granted to negation, to rejection or destruction. A good deed can only be the result of a freely expressed decision in favor of the good *in spite of* the possible decision in favor of evil.

Thus political decisions do not have their particular limits in moral law but only in whatever transcends the possibilities open to them. The area of the possible is thus circumscribed subjectively by the nature of the political agent himself, his abilities and his weaknesses, and objectively by the nature of things and the pertinent human situation. Thus the specific category of political action is not the imperative of ethics or the necessity of natural law, but the realm of possibility. The totality of the possibilities that are in each case available to a person or a community is the extent of their power. "Power" and "possibility" share a common derivation; both come from the Latin "posse," "to be able."* The more subjective or objective possibilities that exist for someone to realize his will, to shape conditions according to his will, the greater is his power. Understood in this way, the concept of power, however, also includes the possibilities of goodness, decency, love, spiritual being. Power consists not only of force, weapons, and riches; there is also the power of knowledge, of love, of humility, of moral law. To see and make use of possibilities, to make possible as much as possible—that is the *art* of politics; the specifically political sense is the sense for the possible. The determination of what is possible and reasonable—ethically first of all, but also esthetically, for example—or what men will consider reasonable: that constitutes the *culture* of politics, the culture of power.

The limits of the possible in political life cannot be conclusively plotted or defined once and for all; they arise from whatever stage of political culture a society has attained or from the society's energy to preserve that culture. Thus the scope of political possibility varies in different times and different communities, which is the reason why in the twentieth century the politics of brute force cannot be justified by the fact that other states acted identically two hundred years ago.

But it must be noted that in two directions the politically possible—and therefore power—is absolutely limited. One barrier is set by the inviolability of each man as a person face to face with his fellow men, which has its basis in free will and conscience; the other barrier lies in the autonomy of fate, which is exempt from political calculations. But even these two limitations are not clearcut, not rigid borderlines; rather they are frontier zones, into which a person may penetrate to

---

*The German relationship between "Macht" and "Möglichkeit" rests on the Gothic "magan," "to be able." (Tr.)

60

a greater or lesser degree, though he will never entirely cross them. At the outset such a thrust into the frontier of the impossible produces an unusual intensification of power when, for example, the danger of economic crises can be decreased by farsighted planning and security measures, or when men are rendered unusually pliable through the application of terror and psychological control. Sooner or later, however, the nature of things puts an end to such successes and wrecks the extravagant attempts at power. Conversely, it is a test of political culture—the culture of power, therefore—that it remains within the measure of the possible. This attitude includes among other insights the realization that history cannot be "made," because it is out of the reach of human power; all that is possible, as Bismarck once said, is to guide the political life of a people according to its own development and historical vocation.

A further aspect of political culture is the refusal to touch upon man's personal core, to strain human relations even at those points where political power would be sufficient to do so. Freedom, justice, and the general weal are cultural values that require care; like other cultural values, they can wither from neglect or can be carried *ad absurdum* through skepticism. A typical result of political culture is the so-called separation of powers, for it is not a mechanism with unequivocal and demarcated partial functions that, once set going, runs its course exactly, but an artful synchronization of overlapping and constantly altering powers, which needs to be carefully cultivated.

Much has been contributed to the confusion and destruction of our political thinking by the circumstance that we no longer know the proper meaning of power and have become used to a one-sidedly negative assessment of this key concept of politics. "Power politics" has become a pejorative expression because we can no longer distinguish between "power" and "force" and therefore understand "power politics" to be "politics of force," which does not concern itself with justice and decency and which has lost the ability to evaluate what is possible. Properly understood, however, "power politics" designates a use of power that, though held within the bounds of justice and morality, nevertheless goes beyond those of political culture. When a party with an absolute parliamentary majority pushes through a law against the expressed wishes of the opposition; when a great power makes decisions without consulting its weaker allies; when a director uses his right to give orders without trying to persuade his co-workers—that is power politics. It offends against no laws and violates no moral commandments; it only refuses to make the effort to obtain agreement with political partners or opponents. It was this to which Adenauer referred in his well-known expression that he was "not wishy-washy in the use of power *(nicht pingelig im Gebrauch der Macht)*."

Aside from the primitive confusion with force, the degeneration of power begins at the point at which it is no longer understood as a method but as the content of politics; where, therefore, power no longer characterizes the manner of political action but is being sought for its own sake. This misunderstanding was already present, for example, when Max Weber declared tersely: "Whoever practices politics strives for power." It is true that a lot of political activity is for the sheer love of power, but it is to misconceive the essence of politics to see it exclusively in relation to power. If a religious synod wishes to introduce liturgical reform among its congregations, it cannot restrict itself to factual reasons but must also make use of political means—that is, it must utilize the possibilities offered by the social conditions in the congregations; it must therefore be concerned with questions of power, but it is nevertheless far from striving after power for its own sake.

62

Politics is the art of the possible. Though this aphorism by Bismarck has been quoted to excess and misunderstood almost as often, it nevertheless touches on the essence of the matter. There are in politics no imperative natural laws, no exactly calculable constructions and processes as there are in technology, nor is there any safety apparatus against all sorts of calamities. All political action depends on a sense of the possible and essential, on awareness, experience, and skill, and on what Clausewitz designated as the fine sense of judgment. Clausewitz described this sensibility as "an outstanding ability of the general in wartime," but the politician requires it in equal measure. Thus, in Clausewitz' text the word "war" can be readily replaced by the word "politics" when he says:

"War is the region of uncertainty; three-fourths of the matters that determine action in war lie shrouded in the fog of a lesser or greater uncertainty. Thus first of all, a fine, penetrating understanding is here required, to enable its judgment to sensitively feel out the truth. . . . Now, if he [the general] is successfully to overcome this constant conflict with the unexpected, two qualities are indispensable: for one, understanding, which even in this increased darkness is not without some traces of the inner light that leads him to truth; and further, the courage to follow this weak light. . . . If this concept [of a sense of proportion] is stripped of that which the metaphor makes excessively concrete and confining, it is no more than the quick sighting of a truth that is invisible to an ordinary intellectual glance or becomes visible only after long observation and reflection. . . . Though there may be no system, no apparatus of truth, there is nevertheless a truth, and generally it is found only by practiced judgment and the sensitivity born of long experience."

The complexity that is as much a part of politics as it is of war concretizes the experience of the uncontrollability of man and fate; this indeterminacy is operative even in the narrowest and most intimate sectors, preserving in them elements of uncertainty. Accordingly, every political structure must remain incomplete and provisional. The attempt to overcome the temporary arrangement and to create completely surveyable and definitive conditions amounts to an infringement of the absolute limits of power and a disregard for the character of politics. This is especially true when it is a matter of creating immutably happy conditions, or of translating ideal conceptions into actuality. A clever Englishman once said about us Germans that we pursue a good thing until it is no longer a good thing. That statement is a pointed characterization of unpolitical thinking and action, lacking in the measure of the possible. For nothing is so good that it deserves to be carried to an absolute at the expense of other matters and especially of freedom. In politics, only the possible can be good—never the impossible, no matter how desirable it may appear. Though man may not refuse to set his course by ideals, the wish to create an ideal reality is irreconcilable with the nature of these ideals (which is that they are images).

Man needs the society of his fellows in order to be able to exist materially and to develop as a person. To the extent that communal living and action serve material existence, they must follow the dictates of basic necessity, and their forms are determined by technical demands. In that respect, neither room nor opportunity remain for the spontaneous, free development of human relations—which is to say, the political. Thus in an automobile factory, the organization of cooperative labor, the distribution of manual tasks, is not politics, not even if each worker is used according to his personal mechanical abilities; for in such a case the uniquely human is only a function of the technological. Political character is conferred only by consideration of purely personal attitudes—for example, assigning especially favorable working places to older employees. Hannah Arendt states correctly that politics and political freedom begin only at the point where worry about basic necessities stops, for politics is not concerned with the preservation of life but with the appearance, the shaping of the world. She holds that an action which must be adapted to the basic necessities of life cannot be freely chosen; only action that shapes the world according to its own conceptions can be free.

When, on the other hand, Karl Marx defines man as a being *working* in society and speaks of man's self-realization through work, he robs politics of the essential feature of freedom. For in this manner he subsumes, as a conceptually necessary feature under the definition of man as a political animal, the basic necessities, which are removed from free decision and which control labor. It must then follow that technological necessities gain the rank and compulsion of political norms, that political life is more and more misunderstood as work— that is, as concern for basic necessities—and finally becomes subjected as a matter of course to the requirements and techniques of the labor economy. All this has contributed materially to the decay of political culture that is characteristic of our time, and it has brought about favorable preconditions for totalitarian developments.

The nature of politics is hard to grasp. It is more basic than factual developments, since it arises from man's essence *(Sosein)* and not only from his postulated aims. But outwardly politics appears secondary because political considerations always gain actuality only from factual confrontations. The distinguishing feature of a politically thinking person is that he sees factual questions from the point of view of their human requirements and effects. Political considerations are added to the factual ones when human beings are affected in any manner. Although political consideration is an element of our existence, it is nevertheless not really a content, but rather a modality, of our thinking and acting—one, however, in which our being characteristically manifests itself. Politics in its pure form can therefore be represented only in theory, while "in the natural state" it appears always as an admixture. In ordinary usage, however, "politics" has gained the character of a subject area among others; it is considered to include many things that may be of political consequence but that have little or nothing to do with the essence of the political, as for example the regulations for governmental old-age care, public health services, or the development of a country's industry. On the other hand, there are matters that are of a pronouncedly political nature, such as far-reaching aspects of family living, to which we nevertheless dare apply the word "political" only in a figurative sense, as it were, because otherwise we would feel that we were stretching the concept too far.

Nor is it easy to represent theoretically the category of the possible that is inherent in the political. For, on the one hand, the possible is that which is possibly real, and in that sense it partakes somewhat of the specificity of the real; on the other hand, it is ambiguous and unclear because it can never be stated with certainty *how* the possible will be realized in any particular case and what consequences will ensue. Furthermore, there are always still other possibilities, and it cannot be objectively determined which of them is the proper one. Finally, considerable subjective factors are also at work: different temperaments consider different things as being possible, different abilities can realize different possibilities. In political action, therefore, proper self-evaluation is almost as important as a proper evaluation of the situation. Often the correctness of a decision is proved only by how it is utilized. Whether, for example, a government should establish diplomatic relations with another depends in the final analysis on the use to be made of such a step.

Unavoidable as it may be to isolate in theory the political in order to arrive at a definition, it would be wrong to believe that in actuality politics is equally isolated. Rather, it is added to the other elements of our existence to make up the fullness of human living; therefore there is no politics without participation of the emotions, morality, and faith. Though calculation is the peculiar feature of the political, the politician does not carry out politics by calculation alone; he also brings to it his enthusiasm, his ambition, his passions, his ethical convictions, his willingness to accept responsibility.

Political action extends over a very wide range of intellectual and existential engagement. It spreads from what is called backstairs politics through sheer tactics to philosophical and artistic participation in molding the intellectual situation of the time, at least insofar as this is done with the awareness of political effectiveness. Equally, political action extends from pleasure at "being on the team," from the fascination exerted by political arrangements as such, to life-or-death struggles. The characteristic traits of the political can be seen most clearly in commonplace political activity, but the substance of politics is found in the formation and the risk of existence. Even someone who prefers to see the art of the possible as a game can unexpectedly discover that it has become bitter earnest. Every political action contains a risk; and what risk an individual is willing to incur is among the factors of his subjective possibilities—that is, his power. Clausewitz emphasized the courage to act in consonance with one's fine sense of judgment, and Carl Jakob Burckhardt, on the occasion of receiving the Peace Prize of the German book trade in 1954, stated: "Sensible courage is as much a basic condition of all ethical action as it is of any mature human relations and thus a condition of the most difficult and responsible of all arts, that of politics."

It is by no means only human egotism, but rather the conviction of having to take up the cudgels for higher values than one's own life, which at times lends bite to political confrontation, so that it is not only an honest compromise of interests, facilitated by mutual good will, but can turn into a struggle in which ultimates are at stake. If nevertheless all are called upon to participate in their own ways in political life, then the seriousness of the undertaking should not be concealed. The idyllic representations of democracy that currently so strongly influence our civic education are, in any case, not suited to conveying a correct concept of politics and to encouraging those energies of intellect and character necessary to participation in political life, and most especially to mastering political crises. "In politics," Karl Jaspers once asserted, "it is a matter of the seriousness of the power that is founded on the commitment of one's life."

Struggle, enmity, the risking of life demonstrate the elemental nature of the political, but they do not define its essence, as was asserted by Carl Schmitt in his famous essay, *Der Begriff des Politischen (The Concept of Politics)*. He sees the properly political differentiation in the differentiation of friend and foe, whereby he follows Hegel in designating the foe as "the foreign to be negated in its living totality." Each actual opposition would thus become more political the more it approaches the outermost point of the friend-foe polarization, and war is held to be the ultimate possibility that lends specifically political tension to man's life.

This contention can be countered with the observation that "specifically political tension" is brought about by the circumstance that man inclines toward and is dependent upon communality with others at the same time that he is a basically independent self—that he is autonomous without being autarchic. Absolute enmity as defined by Schmitt comes about only as one of the final possibilities of this tension; another such final possibility is absolute individualism. Both are forms of capitulation before the "specifically political tension" by the radical denial of partnership. The field of politics is exposed to the constant tension even of enmity and absolute individualism only so far as these accompany the political performer as constant temptations to extricate himself from the strain of politics.

4

Totalitarian Rule and Politics

IT is evident that totalitarian rule and politics stand in the greatest imaginable contrast to each other. Politics is founded in man's personality, it arises from his spontaneity and from the freedom to determine his position in society. The totalitarian ruler denies human personality and will not tolerate any freedom; he wishes to dominate over human beings as over material things and to employ them according to his purposes. Politics is the result of the planning and wishes of many; totalitarian rule actualizes a single all-encompassing plan and elevates its own singular will to the basic law of social life. Totalitarianism does not practice the art of the possible, which tolerates things as they are as the price of freedom; instead, it aims for the impossible: to make history and to create absolutely disposable and definitive social conditions through sociotechnical measures.

It is an extraordinarily important state of affairs, which we consider all too little in our dealings with totalitarian powers, that these appear to infuse politics into all of life and constantly speak of "politics," but that in fact they destroy the bases of politics. It is true that persons are exposed to constant demands by totalitarian regimes and that their lives are touched even in the personal areas; but that is not politization; on the contrary, it is depolitization, because in this way the sources of political life are blocked. Hannah Arendt writes: "Undoubtedly this totalitarian development is the decisive step on the way of depoliticizing man and removing freedom; but theoretically the concept of freedom is on the wane wherever either the concept of society or the concept of history has taken the place of a concept of politics."

Limitation, imperfection, instability are part of the nature of politics, no less than freedom; political freedom must be realized in the face of the obstacles which reality everywhere places in the way of our desires and claims. In comparison to the unfolding of artistic imagination, for example, or of the life force, it is a freedom in hardship. The totalitarian claim attempts to escape this hardship, this temporalness, the risks of the political; totalitarianism attempts an encompassing, once-and-for-all regulation of social life; it proclaims an absolute position, to which must be subordinated everything that wishes to avoid eradication. In both cases it reaches beyond the limits of the possible and provisional into the unlimited and final and thus takes a basic political decision against the political—that is, against humanity, both in its specific limitation and in its particular freedom. It is a *political* decision because it is understood politically as well as carried out politically; totalitarian rule practices politics and denies the political in the same instant. But the roots of this decision are in the religious, for the decision is taken because there is a lack of that faith that makes bearable and even accepts as necessity the imperfection and provisional nature of our existence. Thus it is an attempt at self-deliverance through the creation of a permanent moral state of earthly bliss or of a faith that confers the strength successfully to endure the confrontations with this world. The claimant to totalitarian power wants to "be as a god" and to create a new world, a "new type of man," or to confer on himself a new faith. It follows logically that he demands of his victims—who are meant to be his creatures in the truest sense of the word—the kind of self-denial, devotion, and worship that in truth are due only to God.

In this way, then, the bounds of true politics are far exceeded. Totalitarian rule can never be explained simply by the failure of politics; rather, it is the consequence of man's erroneous understanding of himself. For this reason, too, the confusions spread by totalitarianism, the conflicts into which it plunges human beings, its inhumanities, all are much more abysmal than are political mistakes and sins; they defy all purely political experiences. The nature of totalitarian rule cannot be understood by examining only everyday arguments and decisions, nor is the political history of a people by itself adequate to explain "how it could come about." It is true that conditions in Czarist Russia before the First World War as well as the plight of the German people in the 1920's make it comprehensible that a revolutionary reversal had to happen; but the fact that both people fell prey to totalitarian rule can be explained only by penetrating to the intellectual presuppositions of the political decision against the political.

Connected is the fact that in a totalitarian system the outward form of political demands everywhere conceals questions for man's understanding of himself. Only in time do the subjects learn that basically it is not a matter of a democratic or an authoritarian form of government, a foreign policy of accommodation or force, a socialist or market economy, centralization or decentralization, national prestige or international solidarity, but always only a matter of a decision for or against humanity. Individual rights are not under discussion; what is threatened are the concepts of freedom and justice themselves. Many persons who at first support the totalitarian ruler, because they agree with his immediate national or social aims, sooner or later must awaken to the bitter truth that actually they have opted for inhumanity and have promoted its rule. When they finally understand that they must be unqualified opponents of the regime, and why, they have for the most part already invested so much of their own substance that they cannot free themselves without turning essential parts of their lives into nonsense. This process can be examined in the biographies of many former Communist and National Socialist party members, who often take refuge in the explanation that the Bolsheviks have abandoned the true teachings of Marxism or that Hitler betrayed the pure ideal of National Socialism. Nor are such persons lacking in the temptation to close their eyes to the intellectual and moral exactions contained in the political demands; they take these demands only too easily at their face value and in this manner remove unbearable burdens from their consciences. Such conflicts lie too deep to be simply resolved by acts of civic courage.

Although the totalitarian claim is rooted in religiosity and its effects cannot begin to be understood without this aspect, the religious factor is nevertheless not the source of the particularity of totalitarianism. For it is not the only form of man's self-deification and not his only attempt at self-deliverance; rather, it is one among many, as they exist in all areas of life—in science as well as in art or in love. Rather, the particularity of totalitarianism consists in the fact that self-deliverance is attempted in the area and with the methods of politics, that in consequence it is an absurdly excessive demand on the political. Therefore, though the point of view of religion can reveal the common root of the phenomenon, it is easy to lose sight of the dangers that arise from its special relation to the political. There are good reasons, for example, for considering from the theological standpoint totalitarianism and liberalism as two variants of apostasy and loss of faith; but to leave it at this one-sided view is to incur a fatal blindness for the basic political differences between our free world and the totalitarian realm. We have had the experience of how easily a theologically well-founded but politically blind antiliberalism is seduced into considering as allies of Christianity its bitterest enemies if only they fulminated energetically enough against "spiritual decadence" and the people's ethical demoralization. We have also gained the political insight that the open dissemination of questionable doctrines and amusements in a free society is quite harmless in comparison with a government that bans all these as being injurious to "socialist morality" or the "Germanic moral sense" but that further subjugates society as a whole to terroristic moral constraint.

If, therefore, we take a position against totalitarianism, Christian faith may be able to furnish us with the best basis imaginable; but it alone is not sufficient, since it does not allow for the recognition of the peculiar threat to political life by the totalitarian claim to power. Christianity, moreover, is not suited as a universally binding basis for resistance to totalitarian danger, because first of all it is a gift of grace that cannot be imposed as a duty without corrupting its nature. Nor is it necessary for the West in its confrontation with totalitarianism to find an alternate "ideal," which would almost unavoidably become an ideology. It is enough to recall the inherent connection between freedom and politics—that is, to recognize that we can be free only to the degree to which we live politically, in the true sense of the word.

5

Thought Within the Mode
of the Totalitarian Claim

THE totalitarian claim to power contained in Marxism-Leninism cannot logically be explained by the fact that we are dealing with a closed system of thought. Though the conviction that the world can be completely known leads to the belief that it is correspondingly fully manipulable, the closed nature of a mental construct as such nevertheless implies no claim to practical application. Similarly, the demand to restructure the world according to Marxist perceptions does not in itself contain anything totalitarian but corresponds to normal human conduct. The totalitarian factor enters only when philosophical theory is used in juxtaposition with and as a blueprint for political action, as though man were capable of encompassing the world completely in practice as well as in theory, as though he could rise above matter in action as well as in thought.

The ability of theoretical thinking to comprehend the world in a system—whether open or closed—rests on the fact that theory can simplify at will the infinite variety of objects and relationships and can thus gain a perspective. In each instance, essentials can be separated from nonessentials, the whole from specifics, the particular from the general. This simplification of structures is compensated for by ranking the probability grades of propositions—by differentiating what is certain, what is probable, what is possible, and what can only be suspected. The price of perspective and clarity, therefore, is abstraction—

that is, extraction of a comprehensible schematization from complex reality.

Such possibilities are not available to practical action. Action is rooted in reality; it must accept reality's diversity and cannot fall back on gradations of its own commitment; it recognizes only the one alternative—that something is done or that it is not. Every practical decision must be taken in the light of the ambiguity of a situation, and it leads to consequences that in the last analysis are quite as ambiguous. Every theoretical statement, therefore, simplifies the infinite diversity of reality, while every practical decision destroys the spectrum of gradations of commitment over which theory ranges.

For this reason, though theory can serve as a guide to action, it can never be a blueprint for shaping political reality, and it certainly cannot become a guide to individual conduct. For if the simplified structures to which theory owes its clarity and comprehensiveness are applied immediately in practice, they must deform the diversity of life and do violence to its historically conditioned individuality. It follows that politics will be the more artificial the more uncompromisingly it is subjugated to theory. It is, therefore, this logical short-circuit between theoretical thought and practical action that gives rise to the paucity of possibilities, the coercion and artificiality, that are characteristic of life in a totalitarian system. In the process, it does not matter a great deal whether the theory is correct or faulty, open or closed. The papal encyclicals, for example, are neither erroneous nor "closed"; nevertheless, the immediacy with which Dollfuss* attempted to transfer them to political practice contained a totalitarian tendency.

---

*Dr. Engelbert Dollfuss, chancellor of Austria from 1932 to 1934 (when he was assassinated in an abortive Nazi putsch), set aside the parliamentary, democratic constitution and established an authoritarian regime whose charter was strongly influenced by Catholic corporatist state theory. (KPT)

A special form of this sort of short-circuit is the immediate application of a historical-philosophical system to politics. Man may justifiably visualize the total course of history, its meaning and goal, and he may use this construct as a guide to practical action; he may not, however, shape the details of political life after a law of history. If the Communist functionary nevertheless wishes to do so, that effort amounts to an attempt to carry out the business of the world spirit *(Weltgeist)*. Such a form of politics no longer deserves the name, for it exhausts itself in the execution of a preconceived pattern and loses all freedom and spontaneity. In his *Philosophy of World History*, incidentally, Hegel avoided the danger that man would become the slave of his insight into the course of the world; he introduced the "cunning of reason" through which the individual fulfills the predetermined development of the world spirit precisely by following his subjective passions.

The concept "totalitarian" necessarily includes reference to practical politics. Although the roots of the totalitarian claim lie outside politics and its consequences go far beyond the political sector, it is still properly a political phenomenon. Though this form of rule denies and destroys the nature of politics, the term is nevertheless one of political rule and must be rigidly restricted to this meaning if it is not to lose its outlines and dissolve into unspecificity. Therefore only a particular sort of *political* thought can be called "totalitarian thought"; the phrase does not apply to philosophies that more or less resemble the totalitarian and under certain circumstances are exploited by totalitarianism. For the sake of conceptual clarity itself, then, the philosophies of Hegel or Nietzsche, for example, may not be called totalitarian—quite apart from the fact that such labeling is even factually incorrect. In addition, only in its connection with politics does the term "totalitarian" fit the unique peculiarity of the matter: when a political rule strives to subdue the totality of human existence, it transcends its natural boundaries, and its nature is thus distorted. In the case of artistic or philosophic creation, however, the attempt to grasp all of human existence by no means represents an illegitimate transgression. In those instances the "totalitarian" claim is altogether proper; one may strive to understand, represent, or love all of man, but one may not want to dominate him in his entirety.

It is true, however, that it can justly be claimed about the philosophies of Hegel and Nietzsche and many others that they are akin to totalitarian thinking, make it appear plausible, and are particularly conducive to it—just as all of nineteenth-century intellectual history shows special tendencies toward totalitarianism. For the first time in history, man genuinely gained a perspective over the entire world, analyzed it with the methods of exact research, and carried out a peculiarly scientific and philosophical self-objectification. It was therefore possible for one or two generations to believe in all seriousness that no limits were set to the calculability and controllability of the world as well as human nature. In that period of time, the switch was thrown, as it were, that set the rails, intellectually speaking, in the direction of contemporary totalitarianism.

But while after the First World War science and philosophy already showed a marked return to skepticism, historical materialism and race ideology continued to feed on the scientific trends of the last decades of the past century. To this day the danger persists—even outside the totalitarian realm—that the theoretical objectification of man will turn into a totalitarian claim to control him. For every exploration of human existence and of social processes that make use of exact calculations— whether for objectively good reasons or not—almost demands by the logic of its own methods that practical technological application be found for it. The danger is especially great when scientists simply imagine themselves capable of calculating something that in its nature is not open to exact calculation;

for under such circumstances they submit things to a claim for control that is as improper as it is unjustified. There is, therefore, a recurrent need for pronounced reflection on the nature of man and his world if social science is not to turn into social engineering, psychology into psychotechnology, or the healing arts into "medicine without humanity."

A classic example of kinship with the totalitarian is furnished by technological thinking. For every technical system, every apparatus, is self-contained; it can be seen as a whole, it can be manufactured, it can be unreservedly disposed over, and it is fitted to its purpose. People whose education has been one-sidedly technological, therefore, are easily tempted to want to shape even human communal living in accordance with the rules of technological thinking. They wish to construct state and society after the pattern of a radio, as it were, and they seriously believe that such a process will achieve peace and a maximum of freedom. They are not aware that this would be really nothing but the completion of a totalitarian system.

Hans Freyer, in his book *Theorie des gegenwärtigen Zeitalters (Theory of the Present Age)*, comments on this phenomenon with his concept of the "secondary system"—that is, a system that grows exclusively out of human planning and construction, in contrast to the primary system that is created and maintained almost by itself out of the workings of natural forces. Primary systems are, for example, a landscape—in its homogeneous unity of soil conditions, climate, and flora and fauna—or a friendship between two persons that arises spontaneously from their encounters. The realization of primary systems cannot be willed, nor can their courses be planned. Secondary systems, on the other hand, are products of planning that is both comprehensive and detailed; as, for example, a planned landscape, which is designed exclusively for maximum lumber yield or the maximally profitable amount of grain, or a central catalogue on a punch-card system, or—to cite one more of Freyer's examples—"an express train that nightly reaches the central station through hundreds of synchronized lights, over dozens of automatic switches."

Freyer states rightly that totalitarianism is the specific danger of secondary systems. That is not to say that secondary systems are in themselves totalitarian; rather, they are fully justified as long as they control only that which by its nature can be controlled—over which man must dominate. Only when secondary planning proceeds to include what by its nature cannot be controlled does it become totalitarian. This is especially true when social life—which is a typical primary system in that it grows directly out of man's personal nature and political being—is subjected to comprehensive planning for an artificially produced new society. According to Freyer: "Here there is no taking into account human beings who act out of a pool ready within themselves and which they raise to a higher order, spontaneously respond to that order's demand, according to individual class, rank, and position. Rather, the plan counts on persons who cannot do otherwise than respond to the system. . . . Secondary systems . . . are systems of social order that are planned as far down as the foundation —that is, including the human subjects."

One of the dangers of contemporary life consists in the fact that the subjugation of society under the schematization of a secondary system is a threat emanating not only from the unlimited demands of a totalitarian government, but also from the technologization of the world. Every technical advance forces on human society a part of the conformity of mechanics, for those technological requirements must be taken into account that arise from, let us say, an electrical power supply, traffic control, or centrally controlled food distribution. These mechanical functional interconnections thicken into an ever more tightly knit secondary system that becomes interwoven with the primary system of freedom, of political partnership, of moral and legal order—but under certain circumstances, the secondary system can disturb, paralyze, and eliminate the primary one. The more dependent people's lives are, for example, on a centralized source of supplies, the more easily their political aspirations can be rendered irrelevant by purely technical measures; on occasion, a few technical arguments are enough to convince men that there can be no actualization of a project that seems to them politically desirable.

It is, to be sure, by no means inevitable that the technological establishment intrude into the political universe, let alone destroy it, for the two systems are properly concerned with two different levels of our existence. Rather, the intrusion is only possible to the degree that we allow political categories of human thinking to be displaced and falsified by technological ones—that, in other words, we apply the principles of technological organization to political tasks, give preference to the viewpoints of expediency over those of legality, and become unable any longer to distinguish between judicial laws, which regulate human actions, and natural laws, which establish a specific causal sequence.

Not the least contribution to the stifling of the primary system of political life by the secondary one of technological provisions was made by Karl Marx' inclusion of labor—and, with it, the technical demands of the organization of labor—in the concept of the political ("man is a being who labors in a communal setting"). Nevertheless, nothing could be more incorrect than to be afraid of technology or to go so far as to discredit it, for without it the rapidly growing numbers of mankind could no longer survive. The dangers lie not in technology as such, but in raising technological thinking to an absolute; and these dangers are most surely averted if the spread of technology finds its necessary counterweight in the intensification of political culture.

Besides the modes of thinking and of philosophical systems that are *akin* to the totalitarian claim to power, because they too contain a pronounced claim to control (which in itself may be fully justified), there are others that are *prone* to the claim to power, that succumb to it especially easily, because they have an undefined or noncomittal relationship with reality. Rendering man blind to the contexts in which he actually lives or in which he is included, they leave him open to easy control.

A characteristic example of this sort of thinking is furnished by the vice—especially widespread among us Germans—of *political romanticism.* Anyone who thinks politically in the proper way considers only such possibilities as can be actualized under the given circumstances; he strives for decisions and remains ready to accept responsibility for others and risks for himself. The political romantic, on the other hand, considers a political situation—or even a political impression—sufficient motive to quite casually imagine a host of possibilities that, though they cannot be dismissed out of hand, are nevertheless highly improbable. Instead of weighing the concrete possibilities, he prefers to toy with the abstract, pronouncedly hypothetical possibilities that might be the case if conditions were different. Thus he debates the possibilities that would arise if mankind were to renounce the use of violence, if all countries adopted total disarmament, or if there were a world government; or he ponders the question of what a Christian empire could effect and a Spartanly self-disciplined people could achieve. He submerges peculiarly political problems in ethical, theological, or even esthetic reflections; and, as Carl Schmitt put it, he strays from the province in which the subject in question belongs into a higher one, where the issue becomes irrelevant.

But what is the use of proving from a lofty standpoint the superfluousness of political controversies if such means neither resolve them nor mitigate their effects? While the political romantic considers himself superior to everyday ills, he falls prey to them all the more surely, since his speculations rob him of insights concerning actual conditions. It is therefore characteristic of such a person that—as Carl Schmitt states—he is constantly in the service of other, unromantic energies, and his imagined superiority "is transformed into subservient attendance on foreign strength and decision-making." The totalitarian ruler need only offer esthetically attractive and intellectually interesting material to the political romantic's imagination to easily render him subservient to his purposes.

Totalitarian propaganda owes an essential part of its effectiveness to political romanticism—romanticism concerning the Reich, romanticism of elites, romanticism of revolution, romanticism of nihilism, as well as the romantic readiness of the mass of students of culture to consider everything that is presented in a literarily impressive manner as worthy of political consideration just for that reason. The romantic imagination likes to use even the horrors of totalitarian rule as a suitable background to present most impressively man's "depravity." Finally, the totalitarian ruler's ability to utilize political romantics rests on a more deep-seated correspondence between romantic thinking and the totalitarian ruling method. The romantic flight from concrete confrontations "into a higher plane" corresponds to the undermining of the legal and institutional standards by the "higher" ethical appeal or of the societal norms by reference to the allegedly superior meaning of history or the "vital needs of the nation."

Our confused relationship with morality is particularly open to the totalitarian claim. The ruler would not be able so successfully to misuse the appeal to moral conscience if the conscience were not lacking in the necessary orientation toward truth on the one hand and toward political reality on the other.

If the regime values virtues only to the extent that they produce advantages and release psychic energies, it finds full support in the tradition of our morality, which is far too unaware that the value of the good is founded in its relation to the truth. Our morality has grown sentimental. We no longer derive our value systems exclusively from the truth; rather, we shape them from the emotions, which fact cannot lend them an articulated order but delivers them up to the chance of passion. Often we can no longer clearly distinguish between the voice of conscience and the stirrings of our sentiments. This detachment of moral values from the truth is further encouraged by the conception, founded in idealistic ethics, that the value of the moral act lies primarily in the amount of self-abnegation involved. It can, therefore, finally come about that the totalitarian government causes men to commit crimes by presenting the deed as an act of self-abnegation and the voice of conscience as sentimental sloppiness.

Moral rigidity cultivates a positive contempt for political orientation in that it grants a higher value to words and deeds the more uncompromisingly they conform to ideals and ignore reality. Helmut Thielicke once characterized this rigidity as the mode of thought of fanatical absolutists, who do not know that every ethical decision is included in the political law of move and countermove, that such a decision is not taken in an area devoid of facts but always under particular conditions and within the framework of particular inevitabilities. This morality is helplessly open to misuse by totalitarian rule because it is not in a position—it is not even willing—to consider the political purposes hidden behind the ruler's moral appeal. The government need only present its purposes as a moral good to gather to its side all well-meaning and decent persons—who are, however, politically blind. The regime's claim to control finds ideal points of attack especially in moral scrupulosity. If it could not presuppose scruples in the moral conceptions of its subjects, it could not interpret the throwing away of an empty toothpaste tube as sabotage of the raw materials supply; in the same way, an ill-humored political observation can be made to appear as subversion of military power or the instigation of a boycott, the spoiling of a basket of fruit as economic sabotage, or the absence from house meetings as antisocial behavior.

Another form of renunciation of political orientation is *moral subjectivism*, which finds its satisfaction in the purity of its intentions but does not consider the effects of its activities as a question of conscience. The person who makes judgments out of moral subjectivity is content with the awareness that he intended a good and has remained "decent," while he has no feeling of responsibility for the possible results of his deeds. If, for example, during the years of Hitler's rule or as a party-line Communist he contributed to a ruinous policy, he nevertheless feels free from responsibility by falling back on his good intentions. He asks only *how*, but not *why*, he has served. Since this comparatively free-floating ethic lacks every connection with objective meaningful contexts, it can be incorporated into arbitrary chains of action by the totalitarian regime, and energies can be employed for arbitrary purposes; the ruler need only take care that the subjective balance of conscience of the purely decent person remains intact. Moral subjectivism therefore complements the totalitarian claim to power in a truly ideal way. The person who wants to be nothing but decent finds his satisfaction in being in the clear with himself and on principle gives no thought to his place in society; he does without the basic political decision to determine specifically, for himself, his position in regard to his fellows. In this sense he enters into a peculiar relationship with the totalitarian ruler; for anyone who is so self-sufficient morally puts himself passively into as absolute a position as does the totalitarian ruler in an active way, in that he wishes to subject the whole to the basic law of his doctrine or his will. Thus the ruler and his most reliable tools share a certain mutuality in their basic attitudes, which from a psychological standpoint can be seen to be founded in an excessive egocentricity *(Ich-Bezogenheit)*. The excessively ego-related person has no faculty for partnership and therefore knows only two alternatives: to dominate his fellow beings or to withdraw from them. He does not know that in its nature human existence is always communal existence.

Unpolitical thinking either ignores the peculiarity of the political or brings to political questions inappropriate categories. There are many, for example, who have no concept of the origin of politics in the personal but consider this element as only a necessary evil that complicates objective action and whose influence must therefore be eliminated as much as possible. Everything that is not material is considered nonobjective in a pejorative sense, especially all personal considerations. Such persons tend always to regard the best objective solution of a problem as also the best political solution, without inquiring deeply into the price of freedom or justice with which the solution is bought. They therefore quite unconsciously fall prey to the totalitarian claim to rule, which includes among its propaganda accomplishments the offer of technically and organizationally perfect achievements and thus the sacrifice of the subjects' political freedom.

As in this case, it is evident in general that a connection exists between unpolitical thinking and susceptibility to the totalitarian claim to power. One-sidedly technological thought sees in the acceptance of the typically provisional character of politics a sign of incompetence and lack of efficiency; the political romantic lacks political acumen and a sense of reality; moral rigidity considers compromise an indication of spinelessness. All these modes of thought lack understanding of the peculiarly political category of the possible; they tend, rather, to the controllable, the absolute, the final; in this way they unconsciously cooperate with the totalitarian claim to power. Unpolitical thinking is therefore in a certain way the passive form of the totalitarian claim; it misses the mark of the nature of the political in each separate case, while totalitarianism denies it on principle. The ground is therefore all the better prepared for the totalitarian claim to power the more a people's political life is weakened or even destroyed, the more the people is lacking in political culture and the more uncertain it is in its inner relationship to politics.

But unpolitical thinking can exist only in reference to politics—that is, it is "unpolitical" only where it concerns itself inappropriately with political matters. The word may not, therefore, become a term of invective for everything that legitimately is not political and in fact has nothing to do with politics. Otherwise an absolute would be made of the political, and the independence of the nonpolitical elements of our existence would not be recognized. Technology—in the original and widest sense of the word, meaning the ability to manufacture tools and to use them—art, philosophy, religious life are in no way inferior to political life in originality and are not dependent on it. On the contrary, it is in the nature of politics that politics extensively depends on—and is conditioned by—these other aspects without, however, being able to control them unless the fateful step to the totalitarian claim to power be taken. Not even all human relationships are of a political nature—for example friendship, love, fellow-feeling *(caritas)*, shared philosophizing, and joint artistic endeavors. For to the extent that there is an accord in common experiencing and striving, perceiving and creating, the individual is relieved of the peculiarly political task of consciously adjusting himself to others and determining his precise place in their circle. Such unanimity sees politics not unjustly as tiresome and incomplete—though it is dangerous to be content with the unanimity of a mood where political effort is required.

Furthermore, in the areas of nonpolitical life an intensity of devotion is possible that can lead to deliberate political abstention. By this is not meant apathetic and selfish lack of interest in politics, which is based simply on a lack of communal spirit, but voluntary and necessary relinquishing of community for the sake of a higher commitment—perhaps the worship of God, service to humanity, scientific research, artistic creation. Such abstention is legitimate to the degree that the commitment is genuine. To preserve the right to this abstention is a considerable part of political freedom. For, like any political decision, the basic determination in favor of explicit orientation toward society must be voluntary. A society that is secure in its political culture will not want to do without the inclusion of persons who practice such abstention for the sake of a higher commitment; rather, such a society will recognize in such lives a completion of the political cosmos. One need only think of the classic form of political abstention, which has always been represented by the holy, the area of the holy, its laws and its servants. Whoever, on the other hand, believes himself unable to tolerate the renunciation of politics for the sake of higher commitments reveals a lack of political self-confidence and political culture. It is absolutely unpolitical to demand that everyone without exception take part in political life; overeager democrats should be aware that such rigor gives them a meeting ground with the totalitarian ruler. For this reason the idea of converting the right to vote into a duty to vote offends against the presupposition of political freedom that even the decision to participate in political life has to be a voluntary act.

The reversion to unpolitical thinking, however, occurs as soon as the exceptional nature of the renunciation is no longer evident, when abstention is expected to assume general validity, as though it were the only way of life worthy of humanity, while political life is taken to represent the way of philistines. Whoever, from the standpoint of a higher commitment, sees the confrontations of everyday politics as the results of spiritual and moral insufficiency reduces the fullness of human existence no less barbarously than does someone who small-mindedly raises politics to an absolute.

6

Totalitarian Rule and the State

ORIGINALLY the totalitarian claim to rule was allocated to the state; according to the wishes of the revolutionaries of 1789, the state was supposed to bring about the rule of reason and to educate its citizens to be virtuous persons. When, however, the peculiarity of the totalitarian claim to power became recognized, it had allocated to it social forms that were closer to the basics of life and more remote from the political arena: first the form of the nation as the community of a common culture, later that of the people as a blood community or of the class as a group of persons occupying the same position within the conditions of economic production. This development is no coincidence; for the more unpolitical the determining factors of a community are, the more that community corresponds to the unpolitical nature of the totalitarian claim to power, the forces to which it appeals, the arguments it uses. On the other hand, that state that in its nature is an institution and a legal order least corresponds to the unlimited totalitarian claim to rule. The concept of the state could not furnish the beliefs that the state could represent reason according to which all life can be organized, be the vehicle for all moral education, and finally be an inner substitute for God; rather, such ideas were grafted onto the concept of the state from philosophic theory. It must be said, however, that the state was vulnerable to the extent that the power inherent in it naturally extended to all areas that were opened to it. To the extent that the competency and responsibility for areas of freedom—areas in which nothing could be coerced without their being perverted—were turned over to the state as the instrument of the application of legitimate force, it became totalitarian and itself became an instrument of perversion.

In the twentieth century, however, this totalitarian absolute state, the "Leviathan," is only a historical memory; totalitarian rule is now established in a manner more appropriate to it. The possessor of the legitimate use of force is no longer given authority for the unlimited shaping of society and the education of the people; rather, the totalitarian movement—in its role as vanguard for and organizer of a new society—strips the state of the monopoly for the use of force and claims it for itself. The now fully conscious totalitarian claim to power not only can no longer be derived from the categories of state dominion—but is even developed and realized in explicit and open opposition to the state. Genuine totalitarian thinking is subversive [*staatsfeindlich*] in the most general sense of the word because it establishes an antithesis to a governmental form of state dominion. The state is sovereign and authorized to use force because it represents the whole as against individual interests. The totalitarian movement, on the other hand, does not consider itself, vis-à-vis society, as a part that joins with other parts to make up the whole; rather, it considers itself as the "germ cell" of a new element within the old whole that has already lost its historic right to exist. Appealing to its historical mission and in the name of the future society, totalitarianism raises the claim to sovereignty and wishes to use all means of public violence to impose its partial will on the still existent old society. Again appealing to allegedly superior historic rights, here too the natural subordination of a part to the whole is reversed into its opposite. The existing state, with its constitution and its laws, appears to the power-hungry totalitarian movement only as a tool of its opponents

90

with which to keep down the elemental energies of the people or the class and to obstruct the course of history. Thus to the Communists the "bourgeois" state counts only as an instrument for the enslavement of the laboring masses, to the National Socialists the democratic order of the Weimar Republic was a trick of the victorious powers to perpetuate "German sibling rivalry" and to render impossible Germany's resurgence.

The term "party" neither arises from the theory of the totalitarian claim to power nor does it fit into the totalitarian ruling system; rather, it belongs to the concepts of the free political life, especially of democracy. In contrast, National Socialists and Communists have characterized themselves with particular accuracy when they have designated themselves as "movement" and "workers' movement" respectively; for their aims lay beyond what a genuine political party may establish as its goal. The "movement" is the typical form representing the totalitarian claim to power in politics. To the extent that such a political reality includes a democratic constitution, the movement can also present itself as a party. But it is not a genuine party; the party form is only one of its manifestations. Thus the National Socialists and the Communists on the one hand attacked the Weimar Republic outside the constitution with the methods of civil war; on the other, as "parties," they attacked it within parliament by misusing the democratic constitution. *After* the seizure of power, it is true, the movement can continue to term itself a party in a certain sense if it demands to be the active and leading part of the whole people or the entire class. But that is an artificial meaning; in reality, then, the designation "party" is a linguistic remnant from the time when the constitutional sheep's clothing was still being used.

After its "seizure of power" the totalitarian movement converts the state, which until then had been its enemy, into its slave. The movement maintains that it alone represents the will of a people or a class, and it deprives the state of its existence as a sovereign legal institution. Totalitarianism carries out its politics, not within the framework of governmental order, but beyond all norms, and in this endeavor it employs the state simply as a tool wherever such manipulation appears useful. The National Socialists allowed the state to remain, but they determined its functions to the smallest detail; little by little they withdrew from it its sovereignty in favor of the party—in other words, they allowed it to wither. The Communists removed the old state apparatus altogether and in the Soviet system created for themselves a new one; this too, however, was intended only as an instrument of the dictatorship of the proletariat. According to Lenin's dictum, once the final remnants of capitalism had been razed, the state apparatus would take its place in the museum of antiquities, next to the spinning wheel and the bronze axe. The actual sovereign is the Communist Party, and not the Soviet government. Reinhard Hohn—surely the most significant of the National Socialist experts on constitutional law—once pointed out that in the same manner the state during the Third Reich retained no value of its own but functioned as an administrative and bureaucratic apparatus, which Hitler used as he saw fit. Hitler derived his authority to rule from his position as leader of the people's community *(Volksgemeinschaft)*—compared to which the official position of Reich Chancellor completely lost its significance. The four heraldic eagles on the standard displayed by Hitler as head of the German state were eagles of the movement and the Wehrmacht, but not of the state.

The function of the state is essentially of a regulative—that is to say, normative—nature. It bestows order on a political life that in principle develops spontaneously and freely; the state takes measures only when the concrete situation makes such steps desirable and purely within the framework of the norms that it has established and that it guards. The claim of the totalitarian movement is completely opposed to this; it is of an imperative nature. The totalitarian movement actively intervenes in society and is determined to enforce its particular will. For this reason the *measure* is of primary importance for the totalitarian movement, while every *norm* is considered a hindrance to its freedom of movement and decision. The movement therefore recognizes and postulates norms only when such recognition is necessary for the effectiveness or securing of the measures. These norms, set by necessity, are, furthermore, of an entirely different order from those of the state; they are not regulative legal norms, but regimenting organizational ones.

Corresponding to these differences, the movement apportions tasks by making the state its tool. The movement itself assumes the political executive function as well as mobilization and deployment of the population, and it allots to the state the unfortunately unavoidable administrative work to the degree that this is without political import. The movement itself makes the political decisions and leaves to the state their mechanical implementation. As it was phrased during the Third Reich, the movement assumed personnel management *(Menschenführung)* and left administration *(Sachverwaltung)* to the state. In order as much as possible to avoid open breaks between the political measures (which are not guided by any norms) and the norms (which are unavoidable for technical reasons) the regime outwardly clothed its actions as nearly as possible in legal forms. This legality, however, had no decisive meaning; it served only to bridge the gap between two irreconcilable forms of rule.

Thus in 1938 Ernst Rudolf Huber wrote in his *Verfassungsrecht des Grossdeutschen Reiches (Constitutional Law of the Greater German Reich):* "Allowances for the technical functioning of the judicial and administrative apparatus are the real reasons for the method of legality." But even at that, legality-oriented administration degenerates; severed from the idea of justice and subordinated to the principle of technical expediency, it is transformed in the hands of the bureaucrats into organizational technology for the mobilization of the available human materiel. Judicial decisions become the means of eliminating all those forces that resist adaptation or unconditional enlistment. But all these are not possibilities that from the outset reside in the nature of the state; rather, they arise as a consequence of the blotting out of the state's nature as a sovereign legal institution and its misuse as a tool of the totalitarian claim to control.

This basic contrast between the state and a totalitarian regime is not consciously recognized by most men because it has become so much a matter of habit to view the exercise of public authority as a function of the state that everything that exercises public power is automatically called "state" or at least attributed to the state. Sharp-sighted observers, it is true, were not unaware of the difference. Thus Ulrich von Hassell, for example, at the time noted in his diary concerning the National Socialists: "These people have no idea what a state is." In Werner Bergengruen's *Schreibtischerinnerungen (Memoirs from my Desk)* we can read of the remarkable isolation in which all adherents of the National Socialist regime found themselves: "Sometimes it was almost as if the men of the party and its affiliated bodies were members of an army of invasion or occupation, who had insufficient command of the language of the country they had conquered and in consequence learned little of the conversations and thoughts of the suppressed natives." In the same vein, Hannah Arendt notes that the totalitarian ruler governs like a foreign conqueror, and Hitler himself wrote at the beginning of the 1930's concerning Soviet Russia in a manner that in principle was completely applicable: "Russia is not a state but a world view

[*Weltanschauung*] that for the present is limited to this territory—or rather, rules it." But this was no less true for a Germany ruled by National Socialism! Conversely, it is conceivable that the actual situation of occupation in the Central European countries after the Second World War, and especially in the Soviet-occupied zone of Germany, was especially conducive to the development of totalitarian rule. After all, Ulbricht and his co-workers—together with ready-made plans—were imposed on the Russian-occupied sector of Germany from the outside in the truest sense of that word.

The experiences gained within the Third Reich teach us that under the totalitarian system the state apparatus, because of its normative character, may even offer a certain amount of protection for those who are hard pressed by the regime's unlimited claim to rule—as, analogously, the constitutional order offers to conscience protection from governmental interference. When the Churches found their spheres of activity gradually circumscribed by lying arguments of the Party Chancellery, and when they found themselves delivered up to the arbitrary and judicially unverifiable measures of the Gestapo, they at least had a reliable partner in the state, because it continued to work according to the principle of the legality of administration. Furthermore, such legal guarantees as the Churches still retained were anchored in the legal order of the state and were secured by its continued existence. The state, therefore, at least offered the protection of order as such against unlimited arbitrariness. This is documented by a paragraph in the minutes of a Gestapo conference concerning measures to combat the Churches, dated September 1941, which reads: "It has been shown that it is inexpedient to process political offenses through regular judicial channels. Because of the lack of political instinct that continues to prevail among the judiciary, one has to figure in every instance with the dismissal of the case. In the future, therefore, the so-called agitator-priest *(hetzende Pfarrer)* is to be dealt with by measures of the state police."

In order to understand these sentences correctly, it must be remembered that the Secret *State* Police *(Geheime Staatspolizei)*, in spite of its name, was a "disestablished" police force; it was separated from the rest of the domestic administration—and therefore from the discipline of established law —and was directly subordinated to the Führer and his unlimited totalitarian will.

In view of the different natures of state and totalitarian rule, it is a contradiction in terms to speak of a "totalitarian state," as is still quite generally done. Rather, when we confront totalitarian powers, much depends on safeguarding the purity of the concept of the state as a law-bound institutionalization of public life and on explicitly opposing that concept to the unlimited totalitarian claim to control society. It is a dangerous error to see totalitarian rule as an excess of state power; in reality, the state as well as political life, properly understood, are among the most important prerequisites to protect us against totalitarian danger.

A more or less vague feeling that the totalitarian regime is not actually a state though it is erroneously called "state" is expressed in the frequent designations "state within a state," "nonstate" *("Unstaat")*, or "unconstitutional state." It seems that the designation "unconstitutional state," formed on analogy with "constitutional state," is intended to declare that the regime is founded on the principle of unconstitutionality— illegality. But this concept is not logically tenable; for the mere violation and negation of law can never be a structural principle, and through them alone no political organization, not even the worst, can ever emerge or persist. Thus there can be no "unconstitutional system," only a "system without justice," which recognition then requires the additional state-

96

ment of what other principle, if not that of legality, brings forth the structure; for example, expediency could be such a principle, or power, or technological norms. For totalitarian rule, it is primarily the exclusively functional measure, which tolerates standards only with the reservations of opportunism.

Seen purely logically, the chief distinction between totalitarian rule and total rule is that the former *strives* to encompass everything, whereas the latter has achieved the goal and in fact *does* encompass everything. Hannah Arendt raised a slightly different distinction in that in her own translation of her book she rendered "totalitarian" as *"total"* when dealing with facts and as *"totalitär"* when the term had begun to acquire ideological connotations. In fact, however, the difference in meaning between the two words as they appear in German can be explained historically. Though the word *"totalitär"* can be found in isolated cases in German during the 1920's (for example, around 1924 Hugo von Hofmannsthal made a marginal note in a book by Franz von Baaders: "Totalitarian state Führer principle"), the word in common usage at the time was *"total."* It found general currency especially through Ernst Jünger's essay, on "total mobilization" *("totale Mobilmachung"),* and through the related theory, developed by Carl Schmitt and others, of the "total state." Whenever this concept was translated into English during the 1930's and 1940's, it was rendered by "totalitarian state"; thus Franz Neumann in his famous work of 1944, *Behemoth,* critically examines the theory of the "total state," using the term "totalitarian." For the rest, during those two decades the concept "totalitarian" altered its content depending on experiences with totalitarian systems, its scope corresponding to the influence of the relevant world-political situation. After having originally been used to designate the Fascist regime in Italy and the Communist one in Russia, the concept naturally came to embrace National Socialist rule after 1933. During the

Second World War, Russia was exempted from the category, and its place was taken by Japan; Georg Schwarzenberger, for example, in his 1943 volume, *International Law and Totalitarian Lawlessness*, dealt with Germany, Italy, and Japan as the "totalitarian states." At an American scholarly congress on the problem of totalitarianism in 1955, National Socialism, Italian Fascism, and Communism were once again the subjects of discussion, although as early as 1951 Hannah Arendt had explicitly differentiated between the National Socialist and Bolshevik regimes—as the great examples of totalitarian rule— and the authoritarian Fascism of Italy.

We Germans, on the other hand, though we were able to gather extensive first-hand experiences of a totalitarian regime from 1933 to 1945, were unable to carry on free discussions about them. Thus it came about that the old meaning of the word *"total,"* established in the 1920's, remained untouched by the new experiences and was preserved, while the conceptions fashioned in the meantime were combined after 1945 with the now current term *"totalitär"* which under Anglo-Saxon influence had become current among us. We therefore understand the concept "totalitarian rule" from the knowledge of the National Socialist and Communist regimes and the concept "total state" in the sense of conservative-revolutionary theory of the 1920's, which had no conception yet of a genuinely totalitarian regime. It became evident that in this theory totalitarianism already existed as a tendency but was not as yet really decisive.

The "total state" was imagined to be a state of concentrated expenditure of energies and exercise of power that laid claim to all the material, intellectual, and moral energies of its citizens in order to prevail in foreign policy and in war against other states. But such a purpose remains within the framework of the political, and "to lay claim to" is different from demanding unlimited availability. The claim of the total

98

state, therefore, effects a restriction, not the abolition, of freedom. Its totality is, rather, specifically the totality of the political in the sense of Carl Schmitt's definition, which in this case is completely apt. Schmitt terms political unity as total because, first, every matter can be potentially political and can therefore become subject to political decision (which is not to say that it is available to political decisions) and, second, because man is wholly existentially caught up in political participation.

Political totality in this sense belongs as well to the essential traits of a democracy, for the idea of popular sovereignty imposes on the individual the obligation to lend his energies to the state, to share with it his substance, and to take its part, if necessary even with his life. The (genuine) politization of society and the unity of state and society belong to democracy no less than to the total state, while the sign of totalitarian rule is the subjugation of both state and society under a utopian, unpolitical claim to rule. H. O. Ziegler, in his 1932 study, *Autoritärer oder totaler Staatz? (Authoritarian or Total State?")*, rightly remarks that the total state declares as its particular opponent, not democracy, but liberalism. Insofar as it is antiliberal, the total state, in contrast with modern democracy, signals a reversion from an achieved position of political culture; it is not, however, for that reason unpolitical barbarism, as is the totalitarian regime. Ernst Forsthoff, in his book *Der totale Staat (The Total State)*, published in 1933, holds that the state may not have as its goal the eradication of convictions from the hearts and minds of its subjects by the use of sovereign methods or the extension of its rule so far that citizens act only on orders; rather, it must allow an area in which the citizens may reach independent decisions, so that the state can transfer responsibility to the subjects. The absolutely uncurtailed personal power of a Führer, characteristic of totalitarian Hitlerism, is explicitly stamped by Forsthoff

99

as unreconcilable with the concept of the total state; though the (National Socialist) movement may be subsumed in the person of the Führer, the state cannot be so contained, because it is more than a personal connection with leadership. Forsthoff continues that when Hitler became the Führer of the Reich, he placed himself under a new law.

Such reasoning turned out, in the light of the actual development of National Socialist rule, to be pure wishful thinking, for in the event Hitler did not place himself under the law of the state but subjected the state to the law of his subjective will; nevertheless, Forsthoff applied admirable clarity to distinguishing the theory of the total state, which corresponds to the nature of the political, from totalitarian rule by Führer, which destroys politics. That the National Socialists themselves were aware of such distinctions is evident from an essay by Ernst Rudolf Huber in the periodical *Die Tat* for January 1934, in which it is stated that there was an increase in the voices who considered the term "total state" as an incorrect or at least insufficient definition of the National Socialist state and who defended the totality of the National Socialist ideology, the movement, and the people against the totality of the state.

The true view of the theoreticians of the total state was strikingly interpreted by Carl Schmitt when he called it a "strong state"; in the last analysis, the theoreticians wanted a state that took overt action to better Germany's position in foreign affairs. Junger's essay "Totale Mobilmachung" ("Total Mobilization") demonstrates that in their eyes the concept of totality not only did not exclude democracy but, on the contrary, even arose from the soil of the Western democracies. Junger writes that during the First World War among Germany's opponents, especially the French and the Americans, the war spirit became suffused with the spirit of progress. By proclaiming their fight to be a fight for Europe, for civili-

100

zation, for progress against barbarism, for the freedom of Belgium and freedom of the seas, these countries were able to bring about total mobilization and to develop an unsuspected power to withstand, in spite of great material weakness. "Thus the suppression of that highly dangerous mutiny of 1917 in the French army revealed a second, moral Marne miracle, which was much more symptomatic of this war than was the purely military one of 1914. Thus in the United States, a country with a very democratic constitution, mobilization could be carried out through measures of a harshness that would not have been possible in the military state of Prussia, the land of unequal suffrage [*Klassenwahlrecht*]. . . . As early as this war, it was not a matter of the degree to which a state was a militaristic one, but of the degree to which it was capable of total mobilization."

Germany, he continued, was at that time still lacking in the spiritual equipment for total mobilization, but in future she would no longer be wanting in this commodity. For the war dead had gone from an imperfect reality to a perfect one, from a temporal Germany to an eternal one, and had bequeathed to the survivors an absolute measure of human capability. According to Junger, the outcome of the war was the gain of the deeper Germany, and the new generation—unable to find satisfaction in any idea of this world and of history—sees in the mobilization of the Germans a new form of armament.

In this attitude resides the characteristically fascist turning away from opposition to the ideas of freedom and progress toward a religious glorification of the national ideal. For the goals that, according to Ernst Junger's depiction, allowed for total mobilization among Germany's enemies can sensibly be seen as basic purposes of political action, though all of them, especially the idea of progress, can be stretched to the point of totalitarianism. The "perfect" reality of the "eternal, deeper" Germany, on the other hand, which is taken to be the material

101

for a future German total mobilization, from the outset is outside the scope of the political; as Junger himself notes, it no longer belongs to the ideas of this world.

This idealization of the intrinsically political concept, "Germany," begins as a "straying into the higher," as Carl Schmitt put it in his characterization of political romanticism. The actual defeat of Germany in the First World War is represented as a formality in the realm of that imperfect reality that has no decisive importance whatever in view of the genuine reality of the "inner Reich." On the one hand, this reality is beyond the enemies' grasp, and therefore invincible; on the other hand, it represents the source from which derives the power to bring the enemies to their knees at last. Further, this idealization is of necessity connected with a glorification, and therefore with a totalitarian claim to validity. For if "eternal Germany" is thought of as a *perfect* reality, it must be given absolute precedence over all political concepts and values of this worldly imperfect reality and must have unqualified power of decision against them. Thus a justified national attitude is transformed into the despotism of nationalism, which can allow nothing except itself to remain independent or even neutral.

One can almost point to the line in Ernst Junger's essay where he deviates from the representation of political totality into unpolitical romanticism and equally unpolitical totalitarianism and where, in consequence, the theory of total mobilization as well as that of the total state turns into totalitarianism.

7

The Limits of Totalitarian Power

THE totalitarian claim to power is unrealizable and therefore contains within itself the limits of its realization, as it were. These limits become visible wherever the regime, in the very act of logically following its principles, achieves effects that are not intended, finds itself involved in contradictions, or goes so far as to reverse itself. Its aim—to create a new society and to have unlimited disposal over mankind—is pursued, it must be remembered, according to the assumption that the nature of man can actually be changed. The regime, therefore, does not take into account that human nature will raise stubborn resistance to the claim to control and that therefore a stalemate will arise between the old reality, which is to be overcome, and the new, which is to be enforced; the regime wants a "new type of man," but not one who has been overwhelmed by foreign influences. Thus the regime will grudgingly accept artificiality, repression, confusion—all of which are characteristic of life under totalitarian rule; on occasion the regime may even cleverly exploit them; but they are never intentional. Nor is the depolitization of public life basically willed. If the totalitarian ruler constantly uses the word "political," it is not hypocrisy in this case; rather, he really imagines that his methods of enlistment and deployment are political; for in the same way that "these people have no idea what a state is," they also do not know what politics is.

Thus the development of totalitarianism as such was not mapped out ahead of time either by the Communists or by the National Socialists; rather, it came about involuntarily, the inevitable consequence of the postulated and sustained claim. This inevitability can be demonstrated in the example of the development of a person who makes himself the object of ambitious self-education. In the same way that the totalitarian regime wants to create a new society according to a specific plan, some persons decide to educate themselves to conform to a certain type which they would like to embody, without, however, being cut out for it by nature. Such a person submits himself to a false claim and raises it to a basic law of his life; he places this plan like a grid over his true nature. In order to fulfill the chosen law, he undergoes great exertions and sacrifices and leads a particularly praiseworthy life. He studies industriously, practices self-discipline, adapts himself to new life forms, is constantly alert and occupied. But the greater his progress, the more it becomes clear that he is erecting an artificial personality around his true individuality, that in the process he does violence to himself and becomes distorted. No matter how closely he comes to approximate the outward traits of his ideal, it does not become part of his nature. To the careful observer he will never represent the type of which he dreams; rather—and this is not at all what he wants— he comes to demonstrate the type of an artificial, repressed person.

Analogously, this is the reality of the totalitarian claim to power. Ideal goals (or at least such goals as are sincerely considered ideal by many) are set, and the people finds itself compelled to work toward these ideals with all its energies and self-sacrificing devotion. It actually becomes possible to gain astounding individual successes—and not only material, outward ones, but especially intellectual and ethical ones. But very soon certain totalitarian traits become evident, such as senseless conformity, intellectual persecution *(Gesinnungster-ror)*, criminal behavior under duress. At first such evidence is ascribed by the faithful followers to excessive zeal or to the failure of subordinate organizations. But the influence of the totalitarian elements becomes more and more powerful, more and more letting the original ideas appear as window dressing or transforming them into their opposites. But even then most adherents do not doubt the propriety of the ideas; rather, they make excuses by claiming that the concepts have fallen into the hands of the "apparatchiks" and have been betrayed and misused by them.

Hans Freyer's statement that secondary systems carry within themselves the danger of totalitarian development is true also in its converse, that totalitarian development proceeds according to the law of secondary systems. Invo'ved is a peculiarity demonstrated by Freyer in the following example. A pond in a remote region forms a primary system in that it is a closed biological system, all of its parts in harmony and in equilibrium. If man technically changes it by cementing up part of its shore, or exterminating particular forms of insect life, or planting new species, or breeding fish, he inserts a secondary system into a primary one. The latter, like the original system, is capable of absorbing a certain amount of artificial alteration and can maintain its equilibrium despite these outside interventions. But such interventions can be so massive that the primary system can no longer regulate itself. Thereupon man, who has subjected too large a part of the primary system to his technological planning, must assume the care of all of it. The whole is now at his disposal but at the same time is also dependent on him; it will degenerate if he does not look after it according to a plan.

In the same way, the primary system of the original social order can tolerate a certain amount of sociotechnological intervention. The moment arrives, however, when so many natural ties and connections are severed and so many sources of spontaneity are stopped up that the original system is paralyzed to the extent that nothing happens of itself, nothing regulates itself, except what is planned, ordered, organized, and "implemented" according to the secondary system. But while a natural landscape can be transformed into a planned landscape without basic difficulty, the structure of human society is much too complex and—because of the inviolability of the human person—so original in its essence that it cannot be restructured from the ground up; it finally degenerates into a chaos of paralysis and excess organization. The personal nature of man and the consequent basic forms of partnership and community do not cease to exist and to be effective, no matter how vehemently they are denied and suppressed; to frustrate their natural development means only to force them into areas where they are practically beyond control.

To keep human action and social conduct under enough control to prevent occurrences that run counter to the will of the regime is impossible, not only technically but also in principle. Since the totalitarian ruler is unable personally to supervise each individual and to prescribe his actions, he needs functionaries; and if they are to relieve him at all, they must be granted at least a small area of discretion. But such discretion necessitates a modicum of spontaneity and individual judgment, which means that the area of discretion inevitably is also an area, if not for the free display of conscience, at least for the exercise of the individual functionary's temperament and moods. Because of this circumstance, there come into being factors of uncertainty for the airtight "implementation" of the plan and the limitless guidance of the "human materiel." The more a people is directed in detail as to what each individual has to do, the more carefully his actions are controlled to make sure that he does it, the larger a group of functionaries with discretion must exist.

Thus, even the totalitarian regime cannot eliminate that

uncertainty that is peculiar to every political leadership (the fact that only a part of what is ordered is carried out, and even that part often only in a flawed form); the most that can be done is to transfer the insecurity from one area to another. But while a normal government takes account of man's inviolability in the first instance, and is even able to gain from the situation the partial advantage that the general directives are better adapted to prevailing situations, every independence must appear as resistance or sabotage in the face of the totalitarian claim to control. This fact also supplies the reason why the totalitarian ruler, in consequence of his claim to rule, must be distrustful. He needs no particular provocation for his mistrust; rather, it corresponds to the incompatibility of the unlimited claim to control with the natural conditions of human life. The totalitarian regime must always have in its own ranks "party enemies," "deviationists," or "traitors" because it is impossible for the functionaries to use their discretion without bringing their individuality into play. The more spontaneity they develop, the more efficient is the system but the less tractable as well; the less use they make of their discretion, and if they relinquish independent decisions about everyday demands, the more disposable is the system but the more it also loses its impact.

In theory, totalitarian systems place all their power at the summit, in the form either of the "Führer principle" or of "democratic centralism," while the subordinate posts are supposed to carry out only received instructions. In reality, however, part of the power crystallizes at all those points of the ruling apparatus where there is participation in the exercise of the general power within a certain area of discretion. Experience shows that the summit of the regime is quite blind to these smaller or greater foci of power and therefore exerts less control over them than might perhaps be possible. The gain in power of the subordinate organizations is also furthered by the fact that they are largely freed of the objective binding force of law and of a legally regulated administration. For in order to have as free a hand as possible to put through his measures, the ruler has deprived all legal standards of their unconditionality; the functionaries, therefore, consider established law as binding only insofar as it does not hinder their assigned tasks or to the extent that the ruler has explicitly confirmed it. For the rest, they consider that they are existing in an area free of laws, in which action is taken in accordance with expediency and efficiency. In this way, it is true, the executive gains unique control and impact wherever the ruler explicitly uses the functionaries. At the same time, however, a dangerous freedom arises wherever he cannot use them and therefore leaves them to their own devices. Though in the Communist sphere of rule such a situation may be more of an unintentional development, Hitler brought it about deliberately. He realized that the personal, which is the source of inviolability in the area of political life, is particularly suited to loosening objective administrative discipline and its stringent ties to the law, and thus to rendering the executive organs more open to control. Hitler went so far as to create new bureaus that were assigned no specific service regulations; rather, he directed their heads to take all measures that their political power was able to enforce. The classic example was the office of the so-called Higher SS and Police Leader *(Höhere SS- und Polizeiführer)* in the occupied territories. As a result, the depolitization of public life was paralleled by an increasing depolitization of the administration. Both served to render persons available.

In the Communist sphere, the ineradicable power of the personal is demonstrated particularly in the so-called cult of personality—the excessive prominence and cultlike adoration of individual leaders. It is proper that such behavior be considered and criticized as completely un-Marxist; but the roots lie deeper than simply the exaggerated sense of power of a few leading functionaries. The Marxist-Leninist demand that man subject himself to an abstract idea or doctrine is basically repugnant to human nature; rather, man's naïve orientation to his life shows a tendency away from the objective to the personal. It corresponds to his human nature that man prefers to submit himself to another person rather than to any object or abstraction. At least he strives to see the objective and the abstract personified in someone. For in this way he gains at least the illusion of human connection and partnership—an illusion, by the way, which is consciously and explicitly furthered by the propagandists of the cult of personality. Thus Hitler's altogether personal totalitarian claim to control from the outset corresponded more closely to human nature and therefore was also more seductive for simple persons than the claim of the Marxist-Leninist doctrine. On the other hand, Marxist-Leninist power is attested to by the fact that to date it has been able to surmount every cult of personality.

The realization that the totalitarian regime sets limits to its own development through its unlimited claim to control is no comfort to those who must live within its frontiers; for within these frontiers infinite harm can be inflicted, the lives of whole generations can be destroyed, and man can be robbed of his human dignity. Nor may this realization tempt those who are responsible for the defense of freedom—and that means all of us who are lucky enough to live in the free world—to be less vigilant. But the recognition can help us enormously not to overestimate the danger in the long run, and especially not to feel that we are involved in a lost cause. We are not confronting a monster that is destined and in a position, through inner necessity or as a consequence of historical development, to devour us sooner or later. On the contrary, we have the certainty that the totalitarian claim to rule can never achieve its goal but must be wrecked on its own inner contradictions.

Bibliography
of Works Cited

Adler, H. G., *Theresienstadt 1941–1945. Das Antlitz einer Zwangs-
gemeinschaft*, second edition, Tübingen, 1960
Arendt, Hannah, *The Origins of Totalitarianism*, New York,
1951; translated and revised by the author as *Elemente
und Ursprünge totaler Herrschaft*, Frankfurt am Main, 1955
———, "Freiheit und Politik. Ein Vortrag," *Die Neue Rund-
schau*, *69*, 4 (1958), 670 ff.
Bergengruen, Werner, *Schreibtischerinnerungen*, Munich, 1962
Best, Walter, *Die deutsche Polizei*, Darmstadt, 1940
Buber, Martin, *Urdistanz und Beziehung*, Heidelberg, 1951;
see "Distance and Relation," translated by Ronald Gregor
Smith, *Psychiatry*, *20*, 2 (May 1957), 97–104
Clausewitz, Karl von, *Vom Kriege*, twelfth edition, Berlin-
Leipzig, no date; *On War*, translated by J. J. Graham,
New York, 1956
Forsthoff, Ernst, *Der Totale Straat*, Hamburg, 1933
Freyer, Hans, *Theorie des gegenwärtigen Zeitalters*, Stuttgart,
1955
Hassell, Ulrich von, *Vom anderen Deutschland*, Freiburg im
Breisgau-Zurich, 1946; see *The Von Hassell Diaries, 1938–
1944*, introduction by Allan W. Dulles, New York, 1947
Heydrich, Reinhard, *Wandlungen unseres Kampfes*, special pub-
lication of the "Schwarze Korps," Munich-Berlin, 1936
Hitler, Adolf, *Mein Kampf*, seventy-sixth edition, Munich,
1933; translated by Ralph Manheim, Boston, 1962
Höhn, Reinhard, *Die Wandlung im staatsrechtlichen Denken*,
Hamburg, 1934

Huber, E. R., *Verfassungsrecht des Grossdeutschen Reiches*, second edition, Hamburg, 1939

Jünger, Ernst, "Die totale Mobilmachung," in *Krieg und Krieger*, edited by Ernst Jünger, Berlin, 1930

Klages, Ludwig, *Der Geist als Widersacher der Seele*, three volumes, third edition, Munich-Bonn, 1954

Kolakowski, Lešzek, *Der Mensch ohne Alternative. Von der Möglichkeit und Unmöglichkeit, Marxist zu sein*, Munich, 1960

Lenin, Nikolai, *Ausgewählte Werke*, two volumes, Berlin, 1955; see *Collected Works*, 23 volumes, New York, 1927 ff.

Neumann, Franz, *Behemoth. The Structure and Practice of National Socialism 1933–1944*. London, 1944

Schmitt, Carl, *Der Begriff des Politischen*, Hamburg, 1933

————, *Politische Romantik*, second edition, Munich-Leipzig, 1925

————, "Die Weiterentwicklung des totalen Staates in Deutschland," *Europäische Revue, 9* (1933), 65–70

Schwarzenberger, Georg, *International Law and Totalitarian Lawlessness*, London, 1943

Ziegler, H. O., *Autoritärer oder totaler Staat?*, Tübingen, 1932